MaxAMAZING™
Your Retirement

MaxAMAZING™
Your Retirement

Practical Guidance for an Enjoyable
and Fulfilling Capstone to Your Life

Len Hayduchok

MaxAMAZING Your Retirement
Copyright © 2023 Len Hayduchok

ISBN: 978-1-956220-42-1

This publication is designed to provide accurate and authoritative information regarding the subject matter contained within. It should be understood that the author and publisher are not engaged in rendering legal, accounting, or other financial service through this medium. The author and publisher shall not be liable for your misuse of this material and shall have neither liability nor responsibility to anyone with respect to any loss or damage caused, or alleged to be caused, directly or indirectly by the information contained in this book. The author and/or publisher do not guarantee that anyone following these strategies, suggestions, tips, ideas, or techniques will become successful. If legal advice or other expert assistance is required, the services of a competent professional should be sought.

All rights reserved. No portion of this book may be reproduced mechanically, electronically, or by any other means, including photocopying, without the written permission of the author. It is illegal to copy the book, post it to a website, or distribute it by any other means without permission from the author.

Expert Press
2 Shepard Hills Court
Little Rock, AR 72223
www.ExpertPress.net

Editing by Stan Finger
Copyediting by Makopano Mutloatse
Text design and composition by Emily Fritz
Cover design by Sarah Tenbrink

*This book is dedicated to my sweet, loving wife. Joyce,
I choose you every day. There's no one I'd rather live my dreams with.*

Contents

Foreword		3
1	Welcome to Retirement	7
2	It's Nice to Meet You	17
3	Re-envisioning Your Retirement	25
4	A Framework for Realizement	35
5	Maximizing Your Enjoyment	43
6	Core Soul Needs	49
7	Identity Components and Facets of Life	57
8	Creating Your Identity	73
9	Life Purpose	89
10	Love	101
11	Peace	111
12	Life Goals, Hopes, and Dreams	125
13	Bringing Your Money to Life™	145
14	Investment Allocation Approach and Disposition Allocation Approach	153
15	It Was Nice to Spend Some Time Together	179
Glossary		191

Foreword

"Does it matter how much money you have sitting in your investment accounts?" is a question it has been my practice to pose to retirees at the start of my financial planning workshops. Presenting this seemingly ridiculous question never gets old. The puzzled expressions on the faces of my listeners reward me every time. The awkward silence is typically broken by a brave soul who volunteers that of course it does, but with a sense of hesitancy because I always warn them in advance that it is a trick question. Often, we have accepted that our life's work was to accumulate assets for retirement. This question challenges whether decades of toil in the work force (with financial and other sacrifices made along the way) might have been in vain.

After providing the audience uncomfortably ample time to consider the question and why it might even be asked, I break the tension. Affirming, "Sure, it does-…in a way," I explain why I word the question how I do. I share why it really might not make a difference how much money you have sitting in your investment account and, for that matter, how much free time you have in retirement — if the two do not align with what really matters most to you. It's at this point I have what is referred to as a captive audience.

People have different views of what retirement should look like and varying levels of preparedness to be truly ready for this potentially epic stage in their lives. Most folks figure that if they have the financial wherewithal to afford whatever they may want, and they live in a geographic location of their liking, they are set. But having flexibility with your time and enough resources to fund your desired lifestyle, doesn't automatically translate into fulfillment. Time and money merely provide the potential for your retirement to be as amazing as it can be.

As I explain to my attentive listeners, just like idle time is of little value, money sitting in an account provides no practical benefit to the owner. The extreme opposite is equally true: the real value of a well-structured investment portfolio is wasted if the retiree's wealth is not used for what really matters to the individual -… similarly to dizzying schedules jam-packed with fun having limited value if they are disconnected from whatever in life is most important to the person. In neither scenario is money or time being well spent, and the opportunity to enjoy the highest quality of life and experience amazing fulfilment is squandered.

Your wealth can have greater value when the enjoyment you get from it is also satisfying. Similarly, retirement can be more fulfilling when whatever you enjoy doing also provides meaning. Unfortunately, this is not how many of the thousands of individuals and couples I have met over the years had been living this chapter of their life story — either they're "not doing much of anything" or busily partaking of the seemingly limitless pleasures retirement offers, yet still missing fulfillment. It is also not how finances are handled by most retirees and their advisors. Many simply focus on financial objectives such as accumulating and distributing wealth, without considering the underlying life factors that influence what we want our money to do for us.

As you invest your most precious resource — time — I will guide you through my Life/Money System. We will start with discovering who you are and want to grow into Becoming over the rest of your life journey. We'll consider how Bringing Your Money to Life™ by aligning it with whatever is most important to you can empower your Life Goals, Hopes, and Dreams.

If you are retired, congratulations on your life's efforts and the financial planning that made retirement possible. If you are not yet retired, congratulations for getting a head start on preparing yourself and your finances for the life ahead. True to its name, MaxAMAZING™ Your Retirement provides *Guidance for a Meaningful and Satisfying Capstone to Your Life*. It's a hands-on resource designed to help you think about what an absolutely amazing retirement would look like and what actions you need to take to live it. The first part of the book examines Life and the second part addresses Money. At the end of each chapter, you will find notes that offer greater insight into the content of the book (but could bog you down if you read all of them), and reflective questions to help you consider how to apply what you read to your life. A glossary at the end of the book provides a convenient reference to remind you what the terms in the Life/Money System mean. For maximum benefit from this publication, access the companion electronic workbook and additional resources detailed in Chapter 15 that will help you work through the process of making your retirement as amazing as you want.

1 Welcome to Retirement

Retirement-...the culmination of the "American Dream."[1] It is what you've worked your entire life for, and now, it's here, or if you haven't retired yet, it's just around the corner. At last!!

Everyone knows what retirement is and what it should look like-...sort of. It is when you get to an age in your life when you stop working and you're free to do whatever you want with your time. Between retirement income and your personal wealth, you have enough money to meet your needs and hopefully extra to enjoy the lifestyle you want. You can catch up on things you have wanted to do for years and pursue new interests. Perhaps you will spend time with the family (especially the grandchildren, if you have any), or just enjoy life. Or maybe you won't do "much of anything" and "just relax."

After 30 to 40+ years of exchanging our time for money (also known as "work"), we have arrived at the destination we've being working and planning for. Because we can do whatever we want with our time, we choose to do what we enjoy and is easily accessible. Of course, we all want to be happy and enjoy life, surrounded by people who bring us joy and care about us, as we do for them. More or less, we all want the same thing when we retire,[2] but we may not be able to explain what exactly that is.

When retirement is on the horizon, folks begin to create a vision for what they may want it to be like — starting with where they might want to live and if they may want to move closer to loved ones.[2] They think about how their life will be different and how their relationships will change, what they might want and no longer want to do, and how they will be able to afford their retirement. If they are married or in a committed relationship, they may wonder if taking their income requirements and need for benefits into account, would it be more advantageous for one or both to continue working longer, and when they should start Social Security payments and the pension they are entitled to — if they have one. As they get closer to retirement, they firm up their financial projections and make a more detailed plan. They finally pull the trigger (or their employer may pull it before they are ready[3]) and cut the cord from the predictability that their work life offered.

> Wouldn't it be wonderful if retirement could be even more amazing than you can imagine?

Work could have been stressful and consuming -...or "not too bad." It could have been interesting, enjoyable, meaningful, and even fulfilling-...or not so much. Regardless, it took a lot of effort over many years, and was a big part of most of our lives. In addition to work, we may have had the huge responsibility of raising a family and took time to develop meaningful relationships with individuals and organizations, and dabbled or even became engrossed in personal interests and hobbies. After many years filled with beautiful and trying experiences, we have grown into the person we are and have "grabbed the golden ring" called retirement.

When we retire, we want to continue if not increase the positives and remove the negatives of our life. In our perfect world, we try to eliminate what we no longer want to be part of our life and focus on what we do want. Like a pendulum swinging the other way, we may be excessive in our quest for pleasure and avoiding regimens. We may dodge anything that is a bother or takes much effort, so we can love doing what we want, when we want. If we are adventurous, we may want to be spontaneous and take advantage of new opportunities that suit us, and if we just want to maintain our same routine, we are welcome to do that as well.

The concept of retirement, as most retirees understand it, is a recent phenomenon in the history of humanity. Throughout their existence, humans labored to meet their needs (also known as "survival"), and when they were no longer able to provide for themselves or be sustained by others, they died. Real simple. The concepts of retirement and pension were not introduced until the late 1800s when life expectancy was much shorter than it is today.[4] As recently as 1935 when Social Security was enacted and benefits could start at age 65, the average life expectancy was about 60. People were generally not expected to live long enough to collect Social Security, and if they did, not for very long. The "retirement mentality" we adopted originates from the lifestyle modeled by our grandparents. They enjoyed life for as long as they could after they retired, then passed away. But unlike retirees today, they generally died within about ten years of having retired.[5]

The combination of a strong, stable economy and society over the entire lifetime of the Baby Boomer generation provided predictable employment income to meet their needs and allowed them to save for retirement. Financial markets delivered wealth to multitudes that could support them for decades, post-retirement. Social Security and Medicare funded and protected them during retirement — plus some even had additional pension income and health care benefits. Added to this were the technological developments in medicine that made it commonplace for folks to live well into their 90s. A retirement lasting 30 years is no longer a rarity like it once was, but an expectation. That equates to being alive for almost a generation longer than was true two generation earlier. Nowadays, some people will be retired for longer than they were employed! Retirement now encompasses a broad expanse of possibilities than were unimaginable at the time they were born. Yet, a vision for how to make retirement amazing has not kept pace.

After retiring, we get our feet wet trying different activities and determining the life we want to lead. If something works for us, we may do more of it and discontinue it if it does not. Within a year of retiring, we fall into routines and a pattern of behavior matching our outlook on life. It is not surprising that what we may settle into is a retirement lifestyle of leisure and pleasure without structure that would confine us. Interestingly, even though there is nothing retirees must do when they are free from their previous life full of responsibilities, many live at a frantic pace and share a common observation that they are busier in retirement than when they were working. They don't know how they ever had time to work.

By failing to assess your life, moment-by-moment passes day-after-day, week-after-week, from one year to the next – and before you know it, you are in this place and time, and you might not be sure how you got here. Maybe you just retired or have been retired for a while, or perhaps you are only thinking about it. If you have been retired for some time and are looking back on it, there are certainly things you can view with a sense of accomplishment and others that prompt a feeling of lost opportunity. Considering the many daily decisions that comprise your routines, habits, and patterns, what exactly is it that you do and why? Aside from the temporary enjoyment you experience, how does what you do benefit you and those with whom you share your life? Does what you do "matter?" If you are new to retirement, are you able to project what your retirement would look like in the future if you were to stay on the path you are? How do you would feel about it?

You may be enjoying your retirement lifestyle and at the same time feel something is missing and your life is not as fulfilling as you would like it to be. Reading this book as a retiree you may be thinking your life could offer you more than it is. Or you may be a pre-retiree and want to be sure you are on the right track to be everything you want. Of course, there are those who feel their retirement is sufficiently fulfilling because of the pleasure it brings them. Life has a way of slowly slipping away if we are not watchful. It is essential we actively engage in the world around us and are intentional about the decisions we are making and the life we are living.

No matter if you are working or retired, how you view your retirement, or what the details of your life in retirement are, wouldn't it be wonderful if retirement could not only be all you want but even more amazing than you can imagine? A haphazard approach to seeking enjoyment as the means to a meaningful retirement does not serve us as well as many think and may end in disappointment. As you work your way through each chapter, be open to adopting a strategic, contemporary view that your retirement can be more than enjoyable; it can be a deeply fulfilling journey you travel for the rest of your life as you intentionally pursue whatever is most important to you.

Endnotes

1   The "America Dream" is a loosely agreed upon ideal, meaning you have the opportunity to make whatever you want of your life through your aspirations and hard work. Of course, whether individuals attain their Dream will depend on their values, goals, efforts, and their life circumstances, but they can still enjoy their life, regardless. The same holds true for retirement. Everyone can enjoy their life retirement and exercise their freedom to do what they want in this stage of life, but not everyone has the same personal preparedness and financial resources they may need for their retirement to meet their expectations. There

is great diversity in how people fundamentally view retirement. This can even vary to the point of how pleased they are to be retired, with some wishing they could still be working. Regardless of an individual's view of retirement or the availability of financial resources, with careful reflection and planning everyone can make the most out of the marvel called retirement.

2	The most important consideration for where folks decide to retire is often proximity to their children and grandchildren or other family members and friends, followed by quality-of-life — however they may view it. Cost of living is the next important factor. Of course, there are many tradeoffs when deciding where to live, and some retirees have very specific needs or preferences related to their health or the weather that may limit options they would consider for their retirement home.

3	Toward the end of their employment cycle when they are at the height of their career, employees have the potential to make the biggest impact in their Profession: they have technical expertise, highly relevant experience, insight into social and team dynamics, a strong work ethic, demonstrated loyalty, and business savvy. They want assignments that allow them to apply their unique preparedness to make meaningful contributions that meet their Core Soul Needs. And they want to be fairly compensated for a lifetime of dedication to their craft. Unfortunately, too many employers do not appreciate the unique qualifications seasoned employees have accumulated and are more concerned about their pay scale than the "value scale." They discount what their most valuable assets can offer because of deficiencies in their business model or managerial ineptitude in harnessing their human resources. Just as mysteriously, new potential employers are often more concerned about how long new hires at the latter part of their career will choose to contribute before they retire than how effectively they can contribute for as long as they are employed — which surprisingly tends to last for as long as their work is fulfilling and "worth their time," and not just when they no longer need the money.

4   It was not until 1875 that a pension plan was made available for employees, when it was introduced by American Express. In 1890 Otto von Bismarck, a statesman and diplomat in Prussia, was determined that its citizens receive financial support in their later life. The support started when they reached the age of 70, and when the life expectancy was only age 40.

5   Of course, everyone's life experiences are different. Some individuals had a meaningful relationship with all their grandparents while others barely knew theirs; some met all their grandparents who may have lived well beyond their life expectancy and others never met theirs who died before they were born; some had grandparents who were active and independent their whole lives while others recall theirs living with their family in a multi-generational home and perhaps requiring assistance. It was a rare phenomenon two generations ago for people to live active lives for 30+ years after they retired, compared to the common occurrence it is today.

Questions for Reflection

- How carefully have you considered the non-financial details of the retirement lifestyle you are living? Did you plan them or were they something you "fell into?" Which details of your lifestyle might you want to consider more?

- How could your retirement be better and how would that impact you?

- How is your view of retirement shaped by your grandparents and parents, and by how you observed others living theirs? How might you want yours to be different?

- If you are retired, what about your previous work and life were you happy to eliminate? What aspects of your work and life did you enjoy that are now gone, but you wish were still true for you? If you are still working, which aspects of work and life you would like to eliminate, and which would you want to keep?

2 It's Nice to Meet You

Before we get started with shaping the retirement stage of your life journey, allow me to introduce myself and offer perspective for why you may want me to guide you.

In the early stages of my career, my focus was on offering investments and insurance products that met the needs and goals of my clients. The financial involvement I had with my clients was limited to the financial products I was familiar with and personally offered. This simplistic approach to being a financial advisor was not unlike the approach of the vast majority of financial professionals today. This was the standard business model of financial institutions halfway into the 20th Century: banks sold CDs, stockbrokers sold stocks, life insurance agents sold life insurance policies, and home and auto insurance agents sold home and automobile policies. The more product these professionals sold, the more commission they earned.

Following World War II, a movement began to integrate the various segments of the financial services industry.[1] My personal growth in my career mirrored the evolution of the financial services profession. Increasingly, more financial professionals[2] and industry leaders saw this not only as a profitable business model but as essential to the financial wellbeing of their customers. Similarly, as I grew in my knowledge and skill set, gaining expertise in the different components of the financial services industry, I recognized the need to provide full financial planning services to those I served. I actively pursued the training and necessary credentialing to become a Certified Financial Planner™ practitioner.

The scope of my practice was no longer to match the financial products I offer with the needs of the potential customers[3] I served. Because my fiduciary responsibility was to place my clients' interests ahead of my own, I needed to create a holistic process. First, I needed to establish the various goals of a client and understand how they all connect, assessing all the aspects of personal finances (Generating Income, Building Wealth, Reducing Taxes, Neutralizing Risk and Transferring a Legacy). Next, I'd create a plan that interconnected financial actions and financial products, and implement it-…then continually monitor, reassess, and modify as necessary. This multi-faceted, goals-oriented approach served clients much more effectively than just offering the best products for them to choose from. Still, the focus was on an individual's finances and not the whole person. This required another step in my evolution. Just like selling financial products is an inadequate approach for comprehensive financial planning, solely using a financial planning approach for solving the needs of clients that involve their money, is insufficient for understanding how their money aligns with their underlying desires for how they want their life to look.

For retirees to benefit fully from financial results, the financial planning process must start with an understanding of who they are and what is most important for them to pursue in retirement. This is essential for their finances to "meet them where they are." My view about financial planning evolved into a whole-person concept, and I came to appreciate that money is worth much more than its accumulated value. I saw myself as a life coach as much as a financial advisor and I began to develop a Life/Money System I call "Bringing Your Money to Life" ™. I applied myself to learn the necessary skills to earn the credentials and become a Certified Life Coach. Because I advise and develop relationships with my clients — not with their assets — I see my role as a Retiree Advisor, and not just a financial advisor, and I expanded my understanding of being a fiduciary beyond the financial aspect of the services I provide.

> My view about financial planning evolved into a whole-person concept.

My awareness of money goes back to kindergarten when I remember bringing milk money to school every day in a little envelope to pay for snacks. And then there was the bank book I'd bring to school on Tuesdays with the cash my mother gave me that was picked up by an armored truck to be deposited in the bank. Spending and saving were two concepts I learned very early in life.

A little later, I learned about earning money when I brought the Magic Markers my father's company manufactured to school and sold them to my classmates, I would come home, my pockets literally full of dimes and quarters. Along with that came the pleasure and sense of accomplishment of counting the money, filling coin rolls with change, and taking it to the bank.

I credit my uncle with introducing me to investing, pulling out the newspaper with all the stocks offered on the New York Stock Exchange listed with their values in fractions. He would point out his investments and how they performed. I still remember Natomas was his favorite stock that he enthusiastically tracked. Then there was my godfather, an insurance agent, who made sure my parents were adequately covered. These experiences helped me to understand at an early age what responsible financial planning entailed.

These little snippets in life combined with my dedication to learning and exceling in my studies afforded me the privilege to graduate from the Wharton School of Business at the University of Pennsylvania, followed by graduate studies in business at the University of Georgia, and a rewarding career in the financial services profession.

Concurrently, my faith was nurtured by strong ethics and values modeled by my parents who escaped communism and emigrated from Ukraine to the United States in their teens. Some of my earliest memories in life revolved around faith — praying with my mother before going to bed. The faith that was being cultivated by attending church every Sunday became a more central part of my life when I chose to be a follower of Jesus Christ in my early adulthood. It drew me to pursue seminary studies with plans to do missions work in my parents' homeland. I worked for an insurance company to fund my education in theology, shortly after which my wife and I were the proud parents of four children in a span of six years. I eventually completed my Master of Divinity degree but did not go to a foreign mission field with my young family. Instead, my mission was to serve clients who put their trust and confidence in me in a career that has stretched into its fourth decade. During that time, I have educated, counseled, advised, and developed meaningful relationships with well over a thousand individuals and couples. Sometimes spiritual, sometimes secular, my mission to my clients evolved from presenting the best financial products available for meeting their needs, to offering comprehensive financial planning services, to applying my financial and life coaching skills to each client's unique circumstances.

I have found that retirees can benefit more from my Life/Money System that integrates money with life more than any other segment of the population. They have the flexibility to spend their time and money as they desire and want to make the most of the finances they have accumulated over their working years. Ironically, I have also found that it is this segment of the population that most under-achieves the potential for how meaningful their financial resources can be to them.

I enjoy all types of interactions with my clients, from purely financial to those related to family, personal interests, and spirituality — wherever our exchanges take us. I enjoy not only getting to know them but also to "get them."[4] I love to understand who they are and why. It provides me insight into what drives them, and how to make the best use of their financial accomplishments to help them realize their Life Goals, Hopes, and Dreams and make the retirement they have finally reached as amazing as it can be. Now that you know more about my depth of experience and passion to help, I hope you will be confident to walk with me through the next chapters as I guide you to a more fulfilling journey in your retirement.

Endnotes

1   Earlier in its development, the financial services industry was segmented either by institutions and the products they sold, or professions related to financial services: banks provided banking instruments, investment brokerage houses sold investments, insurance companies offered insurance products, accounting firms provided tax services, and attorneys delivered legal services related to estates. Each of these segments of businesses related to finances require unique expertise (including diverse skills related to interest and investment income, growth of wealth, taxes, protection from risk, legacy for heirs). Financial Planning integrates the expertise in each of these segments into a cohesive approach that includes all the benefits each can provide.

2   The term "financial advisor" has become a generic title. There is a vast difference in the experience and expertise various advisors have and their commitment to deliver what their clients rely on them to provide. Unfortunately, too many consumers are unable to differentiate between more and less proficient advisors, often to their detriment.

3   "Customers" refers to individuals financial professionals serve through financial instruments on a transactional basis where a product is put in place and the customer initiates a service request as needed. Fiduciaries have ongoing relationships with clients where they are

proactive in identifying needs of those they serve and do not base their dealings on selling products which earn them compensation.

4   "Get them" is an endearing term that communicates a deep understanding of the underlying reasons for how people think and behave. It is essential for providing financial recommendations to individuals designed to meet their Life Goals, Hopes, and Dreams that they may not be able to fully understand without guidance from an experienced financial professional in tune with the emotional aspects of financial planning.

Questions for Reflection

- What is your "life story" related to your finances? What were your important memories related to money and how did they shape your views about what you want from your finances? How effectively have your life and financial experiences prepared you to deal with all the many unique aspects of financial planning in this stage of your life?

- Do you agree financial planning is more foundational than having financial objectives and should start with who you are and what meaning money has in your life? Why or why not? If yes, how do you see your values being the starting point for your financial planning?

- How important do you feel it is for all the components of financial planning to be integrated with each other? (Creating wealth, earning income, reducing taxes, mitigating risk, and legacy planning) In what ways is this true and not true of your financial planning?

- Do you want your interaction with your financial advisor to encompass a broader scope of your life and who you are, or be limited to financial plans and decisions regarding financial objectives and instruments? How important is it for you that the financial advisor you work with also has experience and expertise as a life coach?

3 Re-envisioning Your Retirement

So, what about retirement qualifies it to be the capstone of your life? And, what about retirement would make it ideal?

Let's look at the traditional understanding of retirement — when you get to the age you stop working and have the freedom to do whatever you want with your time. In the era when retirement was ushered into the human experience, retirees could not count on having many years ahead of them. They arrived at their retirement destination and enjoyed the well-deserved reward for their hard work. They took advantage of the health they had and made the most they could of whatever time they had left.[1]

When folks retire today with the same perspective their grandparents had, they are also happy to arrive at their retirement destination, but they expect more from retirement. They anticipate it to be much more enjoyable thanks to all the options now available, and for it to last 20 to 30 years. They adopt an attitude of "the more the better" and take advantage of the convenient access to pleasure: social times, pickleball, trivia, cards, mahjong, billiards, the swimming pool, happy hours, dine arounds, shopping, trips, vacations-…. The lifestyle they earned is further amplified by living in retirement communities with other like-minded individuals who share their interests and increase each other's passion for enjoyment.

> Re-envisioning your retirement requires a strategic perspective for seeking enjoyment and fulfillment.

Their ideal retirement is to use their financial flexibility to squeeze in as much pleasure as they can. The result is an exhausting schedule with plenty of stimulation but perhaps not much fulfillment. Re-envisioning your retirement requires a strategic perspective for seeking enjoyment and fulfillment tied to what is important to you.[2] Whereas the traditional Retirement mindset is to have the greatest amount of fun, a Realizement Perspective wants to maximize the enjoyment you experience while meeting your needs to the "core of your soul."

"Retirement" is derived from the French word that means "withdraw" that describes it as a withdrawal or disengagement from work. In our culture, work is an important part of the lives of most people, providing them with great meaning. By withdrawing from work, retirees may also be leaving behind an important part of who they are. If they do not replace what they lost with something that is at least equally as meaningful, they will experience a void in their life that pleasure cannot fill. MaxAMAZING™ Retirement in today's world starts by redefining it. This begins with the vital discussion of what your life can look like when you are free to live in a way that reflects your unique lifelong experiences, values, passions, and skills.

The terms Realizement and Retirement will be used throughout the book. "Retirement" will be used to refer to the period after you have stopped working when you have freedom to do what you want with your time, while "Realizement" will specifically reference the perspective of the MaxAMAZING Your Retirement Life/Money System suited for a contemporary understanding of what this stage in your life journey can offer you.

My term, Realizement, captures a sense of fullness and purpose that the traditional understanding of retirement does not, that is essential for realizing the full potential it offers. The MaxAMAZING Your Retirement Life/Money System offers a way to enter into more than just "life after employment." I define Realizement as "a perspective for retirement, making it the Capstone stage in your life journey when you have unlimited discretionary time to enjoy life and pursue your Life Goals, Hopes, and Dreams while Becoming who you want."

In order to start the process of re-envisioning retirement as Realizement, let's unpack the definition.

The Capstone

This is *the* time-honored, distinctive crowning achievement or exclamation point of your life. It pays tribute to having invested in your experiences, skills, values, and the rest of your Identity throughout your life, including your career, so you can fully benefit from all the free time you will have. (Contrast this perspective to the traditional view of withdrawing from work.)
Note: We will analyze this in Chapter 7, "Identity Components and Facets of Life."

Stage in Your Life Journey

Realizement is not a destination you arrived *to* but a *stage in your life* you are traveling *through*. It is an exciting and dynamic time for learning and growing, exploring, and experiencing, giving, and receiving. If you engage with life, you will not be the same person at the end of this segment of your *journey* as you were when you started. As we know from experience, this stage, like all others, will pass quickly so you certainly want to make the most of it. (Traditionally, retirement was viewed as the end of the journey, not the start of a new one.) This Chapter, "Re-envisioning Your Retirement," is intended to help you appreciate the potential for experiencing fulfillment in retirement with a Realizement Perspective. It will be the major focus of Part 1 of this book.

Unlimited Discretionary Time

Discretionary refers to however we get involved in whatever non-essential activities we choose.[3] *Unlimited* describes the degree to which we are free moment-by-moment to do what we want, when we want. Although we have "unlimited" flexibility, the number of our days has never been more finite than it is today — which will be even more true tomorrow. As we journey through retirement and age along the way, we become more aware of how precious life is. Each new present moment offers us the privilege to make it count for us and others, according to who we are and what is important to us. All the while, we need to be sure our circumstances do not control our sense of wellbeing. *Note: We will also explore how life is most meaningful by connecting to our deepest needs and desires, shared with those closest to us in Chapter 6, "Core Soul Needs."*

Enjoy Life

To *enjoy life* is to revel in its fullness through the activities and individuals we interact with. It is vital we distinguish between quality experiences connected to our deepest needs and desires and those that offer minimal value but add to our busyness. *Note: We will examine this in Chapter 5, "Maximizing Your Enjoyment."*

Pursue

Pursue is an action word primed with intention. Because retirees are surrounded by many options which are enjoyable but might not be particularly meaningful, it is important to discern whether what you are chasing is worth it. Pursue[4] is a present tense verb — communicating a continual opportunity to seize the moment. We learn from the past and should always plan for the future (even in retirement), but we live in the present. You may also need to carefully align your financial resources with those things in life that are most important to you. *Note: We will look into this in Chapter 13, "Bringing Your Money to Life."*™

Life Goals, Hopes, and Dreams

Life Goals, Hopes, and Dreams is not simply a wish list, but a sequence of aspirations for your life.[5] Fulfilling your *Life Goals, Hopes, and Dreams* is the ultimate objective of the MaxAMAZING Your Retirement Life/Money System. You give yourself permission to dream again but also to use your resources and discretionary time to live them. This may be Experiences and Relationships you want enjoy, Accomplishments that are important for you to attain, or a meaningful Impact you would like to have. Living these objectives can make your life truly incredible by providing you maximum enjoyment and amazing fulfillment. (A retirement mentality focuses almost exclusively on Experiences and Relationships. If the experiences are fairly continual and common, they do provide the sensation to qualify as Life Goals, Hopes, and Dreams and fail to offer deeper fulfillment). *Note: We will delve into this in Chapter 12, Life Goals, Hopes, and Dreams.*

Becoming Who You want

Want captures the emotional drive of your interests and passions. Because a ‹want› directs your focus and inspires purposeful actions, it is also empowering. Choosing to pursue fulfilling "wants" is strategic in retirement. As the priorities for your life change by shifting what you focus your time and mental energy on, you will change as a person as well. You have the freedom not only to do whatever you *want* with your unlimited discretionary time, but also work on *Becoming* a better version of yourself. This personal growth results from building into the parts of you that you desire to develop into a more important part of your Complete Identity. (The perspective of growth and personal development is missing from the traditional view where retirement is a destination.) *Note: We will study this in Chapter 8, "Creating Your Identity."*

For a vision to be more than promising, it must be supported by a strategy with actionable steps. We have laid the groundwork for the invigorating possibility of more in our retirement. Now, we need to take steps to make this a practical and personal reality.

Endnotes

1   Consider your health for a moment. Based on medical technology available today, you may be classified as being in good health. However, 50 years ago, you might have not survived that heart ailment, cancer, stroke, or other condition you overcame. Simply put, had you been born years ago you might not have lived to retirement.

2   "Strategic" refers to the intentionality of decisions, making sure they are purposely tied to the objectives they are seeking to meet. In the context of the Realizement Perspective for this stage in life, actions are strategic if they meet the goals of being both enjoyable and fulfilling.

3   "Discretionary time" may be better understood by considering the term "discretionary spending." There are two broad categories of spending — essential (such as shelter, food, health care, and clothing) and non-essential/discretionary (including entertainment, dining, and travel). Just like there are certain purchases you need to make with your money, there are certain activities you must spend your time doing (like tasks related to preparing food to eat, taking care of your health, and keeping your home safe and clean). And just like there are purchases you make on items and services you can do without, there are activities which are not essential that you are free to participate in or not (such as recreation, social media, and general conversation). *Note: this is not a recommendation for how time should be spent or a judgment on how it is being spent, but a perspective on the importance of assessing the value of the activities you choose to engage in.*

4   As we get older, certain tasks become even more burdensome to tackle. Those things we are resistant to because of how we are wired can require even more mental energy. It is vital to be selective about what we take on, so we do not expend our limited energy with little benefit.

5   The longer we live, the less time we have to realize our Life Goals, Hopes, and Dreams. Goals are achievements we have our hearts, eyes and mind set on — specific things we want to accomplish through specific steps within a specific timeframe. Hopes alone do not include an action plan to see them through. We may still have our eyes and mind on them, but our heart may have dropped away to protect us from disappointment. Dreams are one further step removed where not only our heart, but also our eyes have fallen away. We can no longer envision it, but it is still in our mind, without any realistic expectation it will come to pass. But what if we were to hope back into reality and reconnect with our heart to desire it, and what If we were to dream and reconnect with our heart and also our eyes to envision the possibility? What if we were really to believe that not just our goals, but also our hopes and even our dreams are viable and livable? What if we were to actually believe again and take concrete steps to live what we would want our lives to look like?

Questions for Reflection

- What are your reactions to the Realizement definition? What elements particularly resonate with you, or might you disagree with?

- How can this stage in life be your Capstone? What parts of your life do you want to build on? How do you want to grow?

- In what ways is your retirement enjoyable? How could it be more rewarding and more meaningful? Might a focus on enjoyment in retirement detract from how meaningful it is? How discerning are you in being able to choose discretionary activities that most "fill you up"?

- If sometime in the future you were to look back to this day when you were reading this book, what about it might you say changed your view about your life?

4 A Framework for Realizement

Retirement is the great lifestyle "reset."[1] How you go about life — your pace, what you spend your time doing and who you spend your time with — changes drastically. Retirees certainly want to enjoy this stage in life, and I believe most retirees want it to be fulfilling as well. What they lack is vision to realize its full potential for them for what it can be (the focus of the last chapter) and a framework for making it so, which is provided in this chapter. They also need a strategy to finance their necessities in life and the "extras" they want to enjoy[2] Transition to this stage in your life journey takes Life and Money preparation. We'll focus on these as two separate "Tracks" to be ready for the major changes retirement brings.

The Money Track receives most of the planning attention from retirees and financial professionals to prepare for this stage. There is no shortage of benchmarks indicating how much money is needed for retirement — total net worth, retirement income as a percentage of employment income, distributions as a percentage of investible assets, the liquid fund balance.[3] Some financial planners do an excellent job addressing financial requirements in retirement, creating specific projections for how much income will be needed throughout a retiree's lifetime — accounting for inflation and taxes, and which accounts to draw funds from. However, the Life Track is often neglected, and because Realizement is about enjoying a fulfilling life, this leaves retirees unprepared. They step into retirement without a gameplan which could lead them down paths[4] that are not meaningful where they do not realize the potential this stage in life offers.

Both Tracks are accounted for in the MaxAMAZING™ Your Retirement Life/Money System, which recognizes the value professionals dedicated to assisting retirees can offer. The starting point is the Life Track, where life coaching may be helpful for determining what retirees value most, prior to financial goals being established. Next is the Money Track that empowers the Life Goals, Hopes, Dreams retirees want to experience. It may be important to engage a professional financial planner to optimize this Track.

> The strategic error retirees make is not considering their need for meaningful Fulfillment.

The Life Track consists of two Lanes: Enjoyment and Fulfillment. We need to experience both in the activities we engage in to realize the potential of this Capstone to all our years of hard work. With the traditional Retirement Perspective, Enjoyment is the primary focus. Enjoyment is a simple concept, but the Realizement Perspective approaches it with intentionality to maximize it. We will review this in the next chapter. Fulfillment is equally important in the Realizement Perspective and will take up the remainder of the discussion in Part 1 (chapters 5 – 12). Retirees could experience greater enjoyment by being more purposeful, but the strategic error retirees make is not considering their need for meaningful Fulfillment. When retirees feel unfulfilled because "something is missing"[5] in their lives, their default[6] is to turn to more Enjoyment, thinking that is the answer.

To understand the value of life activities we engage in, it is helpful to think about the duration of the benefit we attain from what we involve ourselves in and the depth of the experience. "Enjoyable, satisfying, meaningful, and fulfilling" are similar words but they do not mean the same thing. Their order shows a progression in the duration of the emotional value and the depth of its importance to us. "Enjoyable" is temporarily pleasurable on a surface level. "Satisfying" is more lasting, not requiring as frequent additional stimulation to maintain a good feeling, but it is shallow. "Meaningful" has a deeper connotation while "fulfilling" is deeper yet and has

BENEFITS OF LIFE ACTIVITIES

Figure 4a

	TEMPORARY	LASTING
SHALLOW	ENJOYABLE	SATISFYING
DEEP	MEANINGFUL	FULFILLING

DURATION (columns) / DEPTH (rows)

a greater sense of permanency. As we progress from shallow and temporary to deep and lasting, it is less essential that the element of pleasure be present although it can be, and when it is, the depth of the pleasure is even greater.

The Life/Money System integrates the Enjoyment and Fulfillment Lanes of your Life Track, and aligns the Money Track with it, *Bringing Your Money to Life*™.

BRINGING YOUR MONEY TO LIFE™
Figure 4b

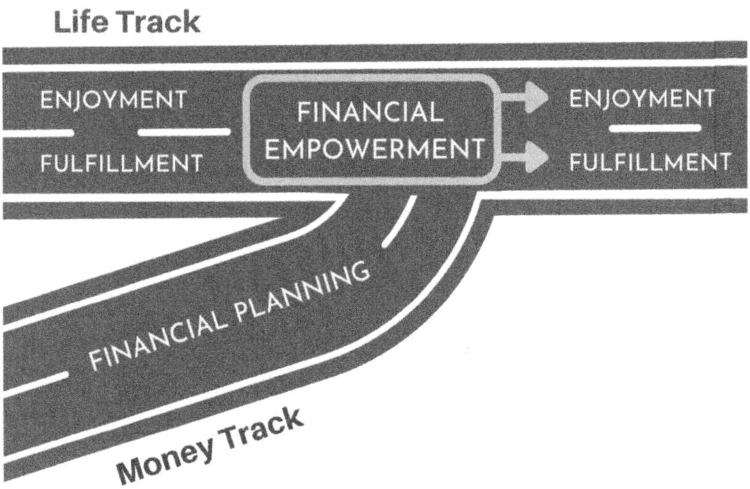

By Maximizing Your Enjoyment while experiencing AMAZING Fulfillment living your Life Goals, Hopes, and Dreams, you will be MaxAMAZING Your Retirement. Let's begin applying the Life/Money System to this stage in life by Maximizing Your Realizement in retirement as much as you like.[7]

MaxAMAZING™ YOUR RETIREMENT
Figure 4c

Maximum Enjoyment
+ AMAZING Fulfillment

= MaxAMAZING Your Retirement

Endnotes

1   The "reset" in retirement includes a drastic change in our goals related to money. Sufficient financial resources eliminate the need to build more wealth and shift our focus to preserving it. Now that there is unlimited discretionary time available, the priorities related to how you spend your time also change. How time and money are spent is much different compared to prior to retirement.

2   Retirees who are fortunate to have enough uninterruptable retirement income (from Social Security, pensions, and perhaps other sources) to securely fund their lifestyle for the rest of their lives have met their need for financial preparation.

3   The benchmark for the total value of assets needed for retirement is of limited value. Financial plans that account for their specific circumstances and needs is what retirees must have to feel confident that their finances are structured to meet their requirements throughout their entire lives. Plans must take into consideration various scenarios and make contingencies for unknown factors.

4   Life is full of experimenting — with something new. As we get older and wiser, we tend to be less bold and choose outcomes that have greater certainty. It is important to continue to seek "adventure" at a level you are comfortable with and provides you the potential for being rewarding without the risk exceeding the potential benefit. *Note: Lifestyle patterns are often created in the first year of retirement. It is easier to develop new patterns that are enjoyable and fulfilling rather than re-establish behavior patterns that have already been set.*

5   There are many ways to express a lack of fulfillment in life, that sometimes people cannot identify: "Something is missing; I can't put my finger on it; I want more out of life." It does not negate the appreciation folks have for their situation in life, but it does recognize that if something is lacking, "more of the same" will not fix it. This helps explain why enjoyment, by itself, is not fulfilling, and will not provide fulfillment no matter how much pleasure is being experienced.

6   Seeking enjoyment is the automatic response for folks who feel something is missing in their life. Whether they are truly seeking enjoyment or looking for enjoyment as an escape from the emotional discord they are experiencing in life depends on the individual and the circumstances.

7   Certainly, there are limitations to what we are able to do in retirement, based on our finances, abilities, and health — in increasing order of restrictiveness. Health is the most severe limitation and sometimes can be debilitating, only allowing us to engage as a spectator. Abilities can be overcome at least partially by expanding our skills or enjoying related

activities that we can participate in. As much emphasis as retirees and pre-retirees place on the important role of finances, this is not as limiting as the others. Certainly, not being able to afford doing something will eliminate it as a potential option for how to enjoy life. However, with good health and the ability to do so many things, retirees who have financial limitations may have relatively little to complain about. If given a choice of having limiting health, limiting abilities, or a limiting financial situation, virtually everyone would select limiting finances above limiting abilities, and limiting abilities above limiting health.

Questions for Reflection

- Is the enjoyment you are experiencing in retirement also fulfilling?

- What specific preparations have you made on your Life Track to experience Enjoyment and Fulfillment in the Capstone stage in your life journey?

- What planning have you done on your Money Track? Does it consist primarily of financial benchmarks, or does it include specific financial plans tied to specific goals you want to accomplish?

- Are you receiving the professional assistance you need on both your Life and Money Tracks? If not, how might you be able to obtain the involvement of professionals that can make a difference in your life?

5 Maximizing Your Enjoyment

The most wonderful thing about retirement is after having prioritized the demands of family and work responsibilities for years and years, your time is truly yours. You pretty much have the freedom and flexibility to do whatever it is you want, with whomever you want that is willing to join you. So, now that you are retired, what will you spend your time doing, given the numerous options before you?

In their pursuit to embrace their new-found freedom and enjoy the flexibility to use their time without the responsibilities and requirements they bore for decades, retirees seek as many experiences and pleasures as they can handle. They adopt a "the more the better" lifestyle and get busy doing things they enjoy. Because they have unlimited discretionary time to do whatever they want, they continually find more and more activities that provide new experiences they can delight in. One day, they may come to realize they are busier than when they were in their previous stage in life. Perhaps this is true of you.

Maximizing your Enjoyment is not about maximizing how many different fun activities you can jam into your life. It is about maximizing the enjoyment of individual moments and your overall lifestyle with folks who make it more meaningful to you. In a way, more fun is more fun, but really, better fun is more fun. The popular adages "less is more" and "quality over quantity" caution against the allure of excess which actually detracts from the overall life experience.[1]

Life is largely a collection of experiences shared with others. With the diversity of activities and people that surround us, there is virtually an infinite combination of things to do with people we are able to spend time with. When we set out to enjoy retirement, we seek things we can enjoy and people we can enjoy sharing life with.

Choices we make are the true test of what we are interested in and value. Since this is the stage in our lives when we can pretty much do whatever we want, we largely do what we enjoy. If we don't enjoy doing something and don't have to do it, we generally won't. (Of course, we do things that we may not enjoy or may even dislike to accommodate people who are important to us.) There are also non-discretionary things we do out of routine and other things we must do no matter how much we might not want to. Then there are things we enjoyed doing in other phases of our life that are not currently on our menu of choices, because circumstances, opportunities, and our interests may have changed. When considering what we may want to spend our time enjoying, it may be helpful to reflect on things we have enjoyed in previous chapters of our lives that we may want to enjoy again. It is also helpful to engage in the world around us — observing what is available and what others are doing that we may want to try ourselves. Most 55+

communities have a large selection of activities to choose from. Additionally, municipalities have senior centers, local newspapers publish lists of activities in the area, the internet provides unlimited information about "what's out there," and word-of-mouth is perhaps the best way to discover what is available. There is so much to enjoy!

> In a way, more fun is more fun-... but really, BETTER fun is more fun.

As is true of *what* we do, we typically choose *who* we do life with based on how much we enjoy spending time with them. This is largely determined by interests and values we share and how their personalities mesh with ours. We distance ourselves from those we do not enjoy and do not want to be with, for whatever reason. As we go through life, we meet many people. Most of the time, our paths crossing is short-lived, although occasionally folks "click," and we begin a pleasant, long-term relationship. Over time, as our interests and circumstances change, relationships fall away.

We maximize our enjoyment when we do what we enjoy the most with those we love the most[2]. It is the best of both worlds: a lifestyle of doing activities we really enjoy paired with the meaningful people in our lives, making our enjoyment even more pleasurable. Or perhaps we should say, we tremendously enjoy the time we spend with folks that make life wonderful, and when we do things together that we both really enjoy, it makes life extra special.

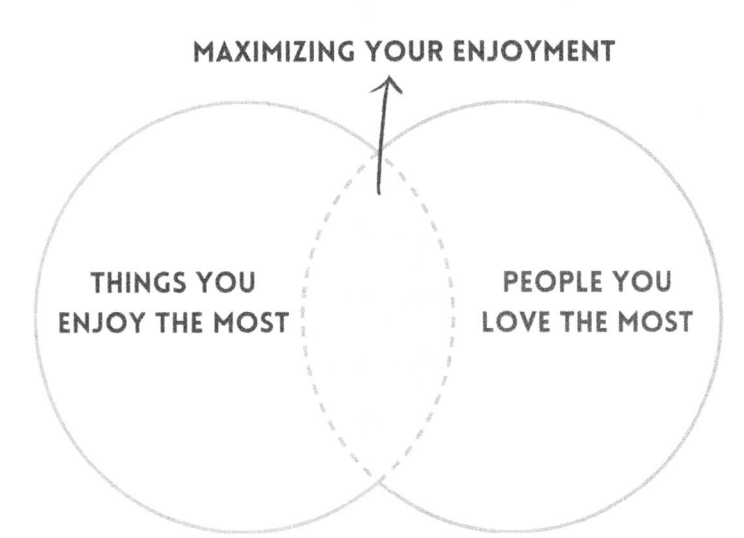

MAXIMIZING YOUR ENJOYMENT
Figure 5

MAXIMIZING YOUR ENJOYMENT

THINGS YOU ENJOY THE MOST   **PEOPLE YOU LOVE THE MOST**

People are creatures of habit, which makes life more predictable but also more limiting. We tend to do the same things with the same people. There is certainly nothing wrong with this and in fact, it can provide us with great pleasure. Still, it may be worthwhile to try new things with folks you currently have a relationship with or to expand your circle of acquaintances by doing things you enjoy with people you do not know yet. For the greatest opportunities to create new connections in life, try new things with people you have never met.

MaxAMAZING™ Your Retirement is about enjoying a retirement that is also fulfilling. By doing the things you enjoy the most with those you love the most, you will be *maximizing* your Enjoyment but that will not necessarily provide you with the fulfillment you need by having your Core Soul Needs met.

Endnotes

1   In the United States, immense enjoyment is referred to as having "a lot of fun," while an English way of expressing it is having "great fun." Certainly, this choice of words is largely cultural, but nonetheless, it highlights an interesting distinction between quantity and quality in how enjoyment can be viewed.

2   Because of different interests and limitations, we cannot always match up doing what we enjoy the most with those we love the most. Sometimes the best we can do to maximize our enjoyment is to do the things we enjoy the most with whomever they would be the most enjoyable, and during the time we spend with those we love the most do the things that are most enjoyable for us together.

Questions for Reflection

- What are some of your favorite things to do? And why do you find them so enjoyable? Should you do them more frequently? What are some things that you do often for enjoyment but do not receive much pleasure from? Have you considered discontinuing them?

- What are things that you once enjoyed immensely but have not done recently that you may want to try again? What options for enjoyment have you come across that you never did before and may want to try?

- Who are some of the folks you enjoy spending time with, and why? What do you enjoy doing together and what might you want to try that is new?

- What are some of your absolutely favorite times when you are doing what you enjoy most with those you love the most (maximizing your enjoyment)?

- Is there a mismatch between what you enjoy doing and the people in your social circle (either because of different interests or a lack of connection between you)? Might you benefit from expanding your social circle to include folks who share your interests, or are there things you may want to try with folks you do not know yet?

6 Core Soul Needs

The overwhelming focus for retirees embracing their new-found freedom is to enjoy life the way they see fit: what they want, when they want. Enjoyment is a wonderful goal everyone should strive for-…no matter what stage in life they are in. What we eventually discover is that enjoyment and fulfillment are not one and the same. They aren't even necessarily experienced simultaneously. In fact, the pursuit of enjoyment may actually interfere with the attainment of meaning and fulfillment.

Pleasure is the emotional elation of the moment. When a pleasing activity ceases, the emotional value of having experienced that life event begins to wane until we have just the fond recollection of it. When retirement is all about enjoyment, which is fleeting, pleasure needs to be reintroduced regularly for retirement to continue meeting our expectations. Some even conclude that a lifestyle centered on enjoyment with the same reoccurring fun activities and even new ones that provide a slight twist on pleasure is "boring." Although a steady pace of repeatedly seeking pleasure can provide somewhat uninterrupted enjoyment, it can mask what it is you genuinely need: deep-rooted fulfillment at the core of your being. What people are really seeking is an abundant life connected to their passions, loved ones, and a sense of purpose. Unfortunately, too often they settle for shallow and temporary enjoyment, thinking it provides them what they want, but it is a poor substitute for what could be the closest thing to "heaven on earth" — deep and lasting fulfillment. The desserts of the retirement life — all the fun activities that are available all day, every day — are the equivalent of going through the menu of life choices and eating enjoyable ice cream and cookies and brownies and cakes and pies and more ice cream and pastries and more brownies non-stop-…and leaving your Core Soul Needs unmet. What you do not need is more fun and games, but a fulfilling, nutritious meal for your soul. What you need is a combination of enjoyment and deep-seated fulfillment.[1]

> Too often retirees settle for enjoyment, thinking it will provide them with what they need.

In order to help retirees be truly joyful and fulfilled, I developed a framework for considering the deepest cravings in people's lives. I call them "Core Soul Needs:"

- **Identity**
    - » A need to feel good about who you are as a person, without inadequacy or the requirement to strive to meet another goal or expectation of yourself.

- **Life Purpose**
    - » A need for your life to have meaning, where what you do matters and contributes to the betterment of others.

- **Love**
  - » A need to be in mutually nurturing relationships with individuals where you care for one another, and both feel valued and accepted and can safely express your innermost thoughts.

- **Peace**
  - » A need to have an inner sense of wellbeing despite the swirl of life and concerns that you are only partially able to control, if at all.

It is essential that retirees meet their Core Soul Needs for this phase of life to be truly fulfilling. All four Core Soul Needs are connected to each other. As we will discuss later, Identity and Life Purpose are closely connected as Identity originates Life Purpose that is tied to who you are and reinforces your Identity. Love and Peace are closely related: Love fuels Peace while Peace increases your capacity for Love. Your commitment to Identity and Life Purpose are strengthened through Love and Peace, and Identity and Life Purpose broaden the influence and expanse of your Love and Peace. For each of the Core Soul needs to reach the potential it can have in your life, it must be interconnected with and promote other Core Soul Needs.

Many retirees try to experience fulfillment through activities that are neither deep nor long lasting and are not connected to their Identity and other Core Soul Needs. The more they move toward a focus on Love/Peace and on Identity/Life Purpose, the more meaningful and fulfilling their lives become.

IDENTITY/LIFE PURPOSE & LOVE/PEACE

Figure 6

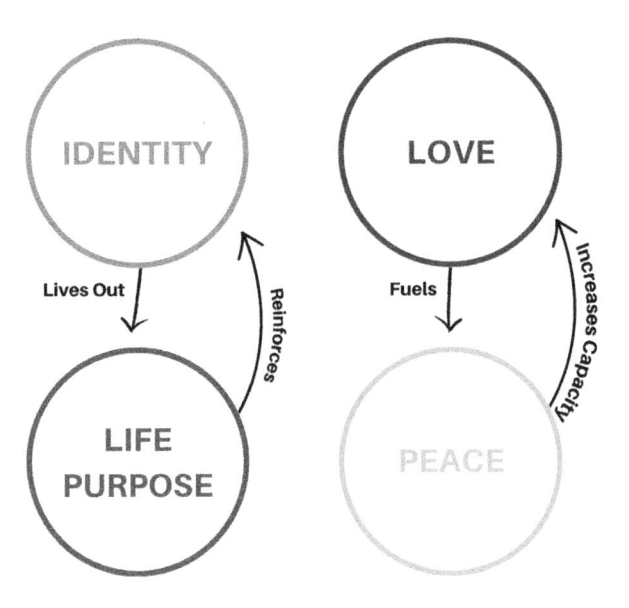

[Diagram: IDENTITY "Lives Out" → LIFE PURPOSE, which "Reinforces" → IDENTITY. LOVE "Fuels" → PEACE, which "Increases Capacity" → LOVE.]

For those not yet retired, understanding the Core Soul Need approach will help you recognize if you are even "ready" to retire. For those retired, it helps identify whether you have the basic building blocks of a fulfilling retirement in place. If not, don't despair, but celebrate it as a discovery. Consider it the starting point for making this stage in your life as amazing as you want it to be. Although the need for financial preparedness (the Money Track) to retire is obvious, I believe we have overemphasized its importance. Too much of the retirement decision is based on having adequate finances in place to fund all the emotional benefits finances can give us (pleasure, security, success, and control). Not enough emphasis is placed on addressing our Core Soul Needs (Life Track) that are important for your overall wellbeing to be met by how you do life. Prior to retiring, your work may have been a primary source through which your Needs were met, but with unwanted pressure and stress, and a lack of freedom and flexibility. Retirement may have rid you of the undesirable aspects of work, but you may have thrown out the "Core Soul Needs baby" with the "employment bathwater."

Work provides the income that is essential for meeting needs and funding discretionary expenses, and hopefully providing an excess you can save for retirement. However, work can also help meet the very important Core Soul Needs — Identity, Life Purpose, Love, and Peace.

When your profession is meaningful to you and provides you with a sense of importance, it helps meet your need for Identity. When the work you are doing is meaningful because it benefits others, it helps meet your need for Life Purpose. When you have an emotional connection either with co-workers, sharing a common purpose and concern for each other's wellbeing, or with those you serve because they appreciate what you do for them, it helps meet your need for Love. And when your work provides you with financial stability and creates rhythm and predictability for your life, it helps meet your need for Peace.

Too often, work is viewed as something to terminate as soon as finances allow.[2] (Work can also be taken away from us, disrupting our plans and pushing us into retirement before we are ready.) But many do not realize how disconnecting from a fulfilling career severs them from what may have provided a sense of purposefulness and belonging. It is often not until they have been retired for a little while that they realize just how much their work may have contributed to their internal fulfillment When those who are not prepared along the Life Track retire, they exchange a meaningful and fulfilling work life — granted, it was mixed with deadlines, requirements, pressures, and obligations — for flexibility and freedom with undefined objectives that might not *work for them* (pun intended). Certainly, their work may have been only partially effective or perhaps was even completely ineffective in helping them meet their Core Soul Needs, and retiring did not result in a "fulfillment gap."[3]

Regardless of your satisfaction with your occupation and what role it played in your life, everyone needs to experience fulfillment at the Core Soul Need level to feel satisfied as a human and for your retirement to be amazing. The discussion for making your retirement fulfilling starts with your Identity and how it is related to the many Facets of life you can engage in.

Endnotes

[1] It may be strange to think of enjoyment as something to "settle for," but the concept of what we want (or think we want) versus what we need applies throughout our lives. People of all ages lack knowledge of perspective to know what is truly best for them, or simply might not

be intentional about choices they are making. As a result, they may miss out on living what is more important to them.

2   When the decision to retire is based primarily or solely on financial preparedness (Money Track), it shows that personal preparedness (Life Track) is not being considered This will likely lead to retirees focusing on pleasure and missing out on deeper fulfillment which they need for a truly successful retirement.

3   A "fulfillment gap" exists when a retiree's lifestyle does not replace the loss they experienced by no longer having their Core Soul Needs met through work. These individuals often look to fill the gap through temporary or part-time employment opportunities in the rewarding profession they had.

Questions for Reflection

- In which of the elements of Core Soul Needs — Identity, Life Purpose, Love, or Peace — do you feel most fulfilled? In which do you feel least fulfilled?

- Which elements of Core Soul Needs did your work help fulfill? How is your retirement lifestyle helping meet them now that you are not working? (If you are still employed, consider what your retirement would need to be like for your Core Soul Needs to be met once you stop working.)

- When you retired, what did you gain that you did not have while you were working, and (other than income) what did you lose?

- If you are retired and are looking for employment opportunities (for personal and not financial reasons) how might you be able to change your retirement lifestyle to experience the fulfillment you are looking for?

7 Identity Components and Facets of Life

"Who are you?" is a more complicated question than it may seem. Instinctively, we answer with our name. However, other than perhaps indicating nationality or gender, your name reveals very little about the real you. Your identity is highly complex and has taken you your entire life to build. As your circumstances and the people, you share life with changed, you changed as well.

Your identity started out as a combination of your genes and the identity of the family you were raised by. As you journeyed through life, it evolved to include various values and beliefs that shaped your character, combined with whatever else you relatedly internalized.[1] Who you are has been shaped by your interaction with the world and those you have shared life with.

At the same time, you have left the mark of your identity on the world through your actions and the people you have impacted. This exchange will continue throughout your life, as you remain relevant to the world around you.

> The more important your Profession was as part of your Identity, the larger the void you will experience in its absence.

Who you are (your "Complete Identity") is a combination of your Belief/Values/Character and multiple Identity Components. In this chapter, I share a structure to help you think about who you are, what is important to you, and what your life could look like. This structure is not definitive or prescriptive for all areas of everyone's life.

Identity Components

- Appearance
    - » The most evident part of your Identity since it can be visually observed by others instantaneously. It may contribute to a positive or negative[2] view of yourself, possibly influenced by the judgmental values of others and society that you believe are valid and you internalize.

- Physique
    - » The physical and genetic part of your identity directly tied to functionality, including your health and the physical attributes that are inseparable from you. You may be able to affect some of them to some extent by diet, exercise, and life choices.[3]

- Family
    - » Your nuclear family (your parents/siblings when you were a child, and your spouse/children if you've had them). It also includes your

extended family to a lesser extent. This group of individuals who lived in your home are usually the dearest people in your life. When you are an empty nester, your responsibilities lessen and your primary Identity within the family may change from parent to grandparent.

- **Profession**
  - » Your employment (with an employer or your own company) where you spent as much as a third or more of your waking hours. It is what you did to support yourself and your loved ones and may have dictated your standard of living and where you resided geographically. It could also have been a place of social connectedness and affirmed you with success and recognition, while also being your primary source of stress.

- **Community**
  - » Individuals you share a connection with due to something you have in common, whether nationality, ethnicity, civic and social affiliations, residence, and interests that create a sense of "belonging." Those with whom you associate can reinforce, influence, or even bring about change in you as a person. Over time, you, and those you associate with, will become more similar as you "rub off on each other."

- **Intellect/Abilities**
    - » Your mental capabilities and what you know, combined with the accumulated skills you have a command of that allow you to conceptualize and assimilate information and accomplish tasks.

- **Avocation**
    - » The interests you pursue with a commitment of time and resources because of your passion and the importance you place on them.

- **Wealth**
    - » A measure of the economic power you have to purchase goods and services. Depending on the importance you place on money and what it is you want your money to accomplish for you, how you view yourself can be affected by your financial situation and what it empowers you to do, often compared to others.

- **Faith**
    - » Your beliefs and awareness of a meaningful non-material realm which shapes how you approach life and prioritize the material world.

Your Identity is who you see yourself to be. It can derive from reality, what others have said about you that you believe, or simply what you want to be true of you. The combination of objective, accepted and self-created Identity is the sum of what you have observed, processed, and internalized that you believe represents who you are. What you choose to do largely stems from your Identity.

Naturally, as a part of society, you do many things and have various points of interaction with the world around you. You may have Descriptors in your life that tell what you are doing, but these do not tie into your Identity until they are internalized. They describe what you do and not who you are — like watch TV or go for a walk. Watching TV does not make you a "TV-watcher" and going for a walk does not make you a "walker." These are actions that you have limited interest in and engage in with a low level of commitment. You may also do them infrequently. Activities do not become part of your identity until they become so important to you that you identify yourself with them and doing them is an expression of who you are. This happens after your interest in the action has grown beyond simply being actions and you develop a passion and prioritize that part of your life.

Your Beliefs/Values/Character are the foundation of who you are and serve as a filter through which everything in your life is screened. This impacts everything that is true about you and is reflected by your moral and ethical views. This filter establishes your perspective on the world showing what you feel is important, your preferences, what you are like and how you do life. You will allow Identity Components to be part of you only if they square with your Beliefs/Values/Character. Anything that you may want to adopt as part of your Identity that may be inconstant with your B/V/C, will be rejected or will require you to change at this deep level of who you are before it can be part of your Complete Identity.

BELIEFS/VALUES/CHARACTER

Figure 7a

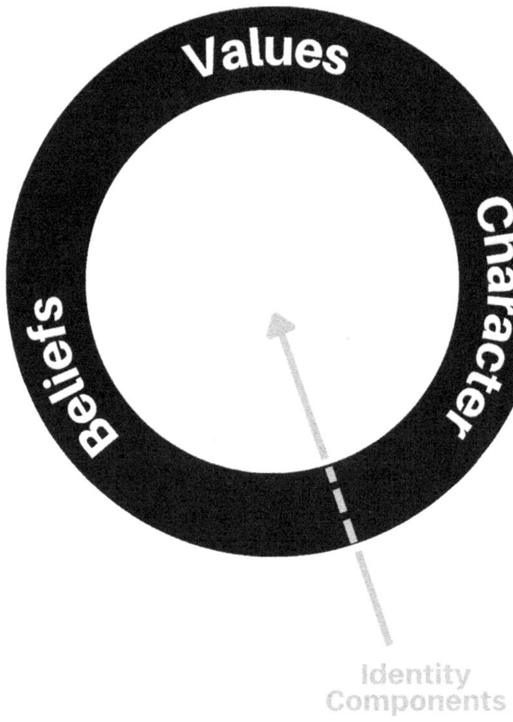

Identity Components have varying levels of importance in making up your Complete Identity. Within your Complete Identity you will have a Chief Identity. It could be a single Identity Component, or your Beliefs and Values can serve as a Chief Identity that several Identity Components cluster around. You can tell something is your Identity if it is what you prefer to spend your time doing and is a frequent or even constant focus of your thoughts. It is the "go-to" part of your life you seek to meet your emotional needs, particularly when you are feeling undesirable emotions such as worry, anxiety, stress, loneliness. The more important it is to you, the more time you spend pursuing and "living it," and with greater the intensity, to the point it can be consuming. If it were to stop being part of your life you would feel a great loss as if an important part of you died.

IDENTITY COMPONENTS & FACETS OF LIFE

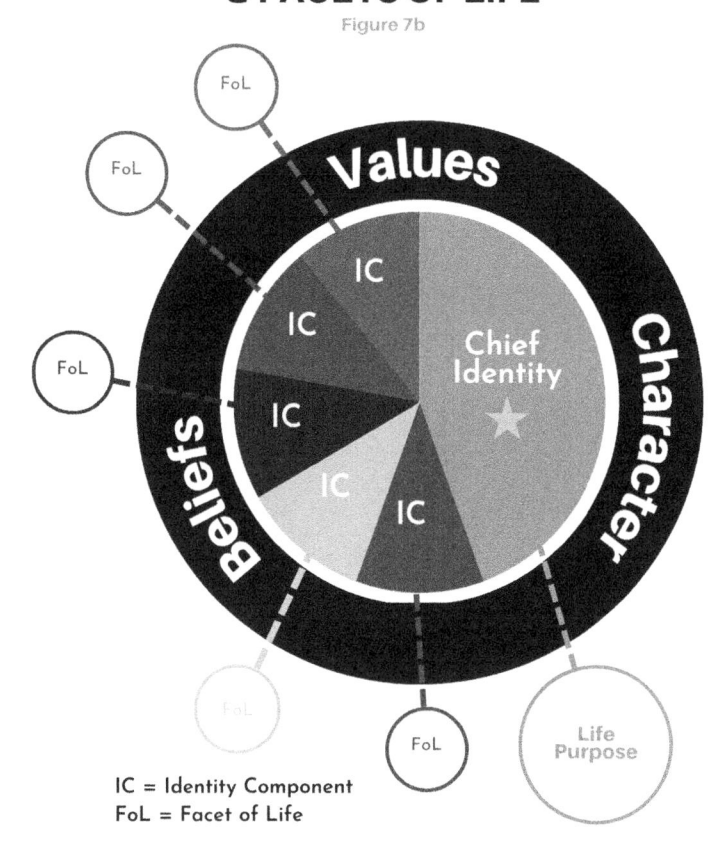

Figure 7b

IC = Identity Component
FoL = Facet of Life

If your Chief Identity is a single Identity Component, your life will focus on that fairly narrow part of who you are — a sole focus you may have a great passion about. If your Chief Identity is a cluster of Identity Components, they will be linked by an aspect of your Beliefs/Values/Character. It could include a Belief or Value (such as your faith or a cause) that is so important to you that it pervades many parts of your life. It could also be part of your Character, perhaps shaped by defining moments in life. You may have come to instinctively incorporate aspects of your Character that are so important to you that they largely determine how do life and what you choose to do. For example, you may be accomplishment-oriented and want (or need) to succeed in all parts of your life. Or you may be compassionate and feel drawn to a concern for everyone through whatever you are involved in. This Chief Identity may continually be looking for opportunities to be compassionate to others and express yourself through many of your Identity Components.

To have a framework for thinking about how important the seemingly unlimited variety of activities are to you and how you may want to spend your time, it is helpful to think in terms of categories or Facets of Life. When you retire, Work is no longer a Facet of Life retirees can engage in, but it is included in the list.

Facets of Life

- **Cosmetic Improvements**
    - » Making yourself look more attractive to feel better about who you are and influence how you think others will evaluate and value you based on your appearance.[5]

- Health/Wellness
  - » Taking care of your body through medical attention, fitness, nutrition, and life habits to extend your longevity and improve your lifestyle.

- Family Involvement
  - » Spending time with parents, siblings, children, and grandchildren and also extended family to enjoy each other, make memories, and build into younger generations.

- Work
  - » Performing duties requiring skill and experience that are integrated with society and the economy as an employee of a firm or the owner of your own, primarily to earn income but also for enjoyment and fulfillment.

- Association/Relationships
  - » Connecting with individuals or groups with whom you share a mutual interest that provides comradery.

- Knowledge/Skills
  - » Gaining information and learning about topics of interest to you and how to do things that are important for you to be more effective.

- **Hobbies/Volunteering**
    - » Applying yourself to pastimes or causes you love with a commitment, for the benefit they provide you.

- **Finances**
    - » Improving financial outcomes by growing or structuring wealth so your money becomes more valuable, either by amassing it or by what it achieves or allows you to do.

- **Spirituality**
    - » Engaging life in a way you believe is not fully experienced in the material realm, for purposes and benefits the physical world is unable to provide sufficiently if at all.

- **Recreation**
    - » Participating in pleasurable activities because of the enjoyment they bring or the stimulation and refreshment they provide.

When you retire and no longer have a prescribed structure for your life, it is important to establish a Life Rhythm for your routine to provide you with predictability and greater purposefulness. Otherwise, every day will "feel like a Saturday" without any particular importance for that day or things you set your mind on doing to make the most of it.

Facet of Life activities in which we engage with a degree of regularity or commitment are likely to be Identity-based, flowing from *who we are*. Passing interests that we have not prioritized highly enough to identify with or are not consistent with our Beliefs/Values/Character are merely Descriptors that say something *about us*. For example, playing golf is a Hobby (Facet of Life activity) stemming from someone who has an Avocation (Identity) of being a golfer. Because golf is not just something they do but an expression of who they are, it is not merely a passing interest. In addition to spending time on the golf course, they are likely to read magazines about it, watch golf tournaments, take care of their clubs, and associate with others who also identify as golfers. The more important this Component is, the more it permeates their life and fills their thoughts and actions — to the point of possibly "obsessing" with it if it is a key part of their Chief Identity. The more they engage with it, the more golf is reinforced as an Identity and increases in importance in their life. Compare this to someone who plays golf once a year. It is unlikely this person would self-identify as a golfer. Instead, playing golf would be a Descriptor of this individual. For something truly to be a significant part of you, you would more than have to *do it* — you would have to *be it*.

There is a close correspondence between the Identity Components (who you are) and Facets of Life (what you do) — which makes sense because you express who you are by what you do. It is easy to see which Identity Components most of the Facets of Life Feed and grow you into Becoming, given enough time and perhaps[6] effort:

Facet of Life	Feeds[7]	Identity Component
Cosmetic Improvements	→	Physical Appearance
Health/Wellness	→	Physique
Family Involvement	→	Family
Work	→	Profession
Association/Relationships	→	Community
Knowledge/Skills	→	Intellect/Abilities
Hobbies/Volunteering	→	Avocation
Finances	→	Wealth
Spirituality	→	Faith

When people retire, Work is no longer an active Facet of Life for them, but if their Profession was sufficiently important for them to identify with it, it does not automatically cease being part of their Identity. They may hold onto it as a part of who they are, but they can no longer Feed it. This creates a disconnection between what they are able to do and who they still see themselves as "being" that diminishes over time.

Facet of Life	Cannot Feed	Identity Component
Work (Discontinued for Retirees)	X	Profession (retired)

The more important your Profession was as part of your Identity — and it may have been your Chief Identity — the larger the void you will experience in its absence. The way to know if your Profession or anything about you is central to your Identity and not just a Descriptor is if eliminating it from your life creates a feeling of emptiness and a loss of part of you. Losing an Identity may result in a sense of depression and "feeling lost" and a need for something meaningful to replace it. Regardless of what your Identity Components were while you were employed or how important they were, you can work on creating a fulfilling Identity in your retirement as part of a process of Becoming who you want.

Endnotes

1   Whether a belief or value, activity, cause, organization, relationship, perspective, emotion, idea, etc., when we internalize anything in life, we simultaneously identify with it as a part of who we are. It affects what we say and do, and even think. When we identify with something or internalize it, it becomes part of our Beliefs/Values/Character through

which we filter everything. We choose what to potentially allow to become part of our lives — even determining whether to expose ourselves to something or someone in the first place.

2   Positive and negative assessments of physical appearance are highly subjective, based on varying cultural standards that change over time. Individuals have the freedom to accept or reject the subjective assessments of their physical appearance and need not internalize them as part of their Identity.

3   Your physique is inseparable from who you are, but you choose whether to internalize it as a core part of your Identity or merely acknowledge it as a Descriptor of your physical appearance. By internalizing it, you agree that your appearance defines you in part. By rejecting it as part of your Identity, you are not denying its existence, but allowing it simply to describe who you are. Using a ridiculous example to make a point that would not be offensive to anyone, let's say you were to have two heads, which may be perceived as an undesirable trait. You could view your Identity as a three-headed person or a person who is described as having two heads. You could accept or reject three heads as central to your Identity without denying you have three heads, regardless of how others may view you and may want to identify you.

4   For some individuals, the prestige associated with the figurehead may be more important than the requirements and responsibilities of the role.

5   If you view your Physical Appearance as being part of your Identity, Cosmetic Improvements may be a way to change who you are. People are free to order their life how they want, but identifying with your appearance and having a deep need to change how you look to become a different person may bind who you are to how you look. If you choose to make your Appearance an Identity Component, by changing your Appearance you change who you are. If you should be unable to change your Appearance that you view as part of who you are,

you will be unable to change as a person. (Likewise, you will not be able to maintain an Appearance-based identity when your appearance cannot be maintained/restored to past standards). It is not an overstatement to say this mindset takes your Identity out of your control; it exposes you to others determining your worth based on your reaction to their assessment of Your Appearance.

6   Engaging in Facets of Life might require dedication, or it may be fairly effortless, depending on the nature of the activity and the level of commitment we are willing to extend. Regardless of what it is we do, the Facets of Life we engage in build into our Identity simultaneously and automatically, without requiring any additional effort — whether we realize it or even want it to.

7   The Facets of Life you engage in "Feed Into" an Identity Component. The longer you engage in an activity and with heavier intensity, the greater the meaning it will have in your life, and the more it will impact your Identity Component associated with it. If a Facet of Life stems from what is already an Identity Component, engaging in it will reinforce its importance to you — either maintaining or growing its level of importance.

Questions for Reflection

- Which of the Identity Components are the most important to you?

- What would you say is your Chief Identity? Is it a single Component or a Belief or Value that other Identity Components cluster around? Can you remember recent instances when you turned to your Chief Identity to have your emotional needs met? (There should be many.)

- How important was your Profession to you as a part of your identity when you were working? Does being retired cause you to feel a loss in your Identity that you may want to fill with another Identity Component? If your Profession was your Chief Identity, how are you going about replacing it?

- In which parts of your Identity would you like to grow positively? Are you currently reflecting on any aspects of your Beliefs/Values/Character? Are there any you should be?

- Are there new Facets of Life you may want to connect with or Facets of Life you may want to reconnect with that were previously important, but you have not engaged in recently?

8 Creating Your Identity

"Retiree" is how someone who has "permanently" exited the workforce is referred to. It describes who they *are not* (their ex-Profession), but it does not say what they are doing or more importantly, who they *are* at this stage in their life.

Upon retirement, folks immediately gain a new Descriptor as a *retiree*, but not a new Identity. By identifying as being retired, their point of reference is a *previous* Identity — their ex-Profession — who they no longer are. We have become accustomed to think about ourselves as retirees, but if you think about it, it would be odd to have a new neighbor introduce themselves as someone who they no longer are: "Hi, I'm not-an-electrician and this is my wife, no-longer-on the town council. I stopped being an avid sports fans and she stopped being in the Rotary Club." Because *retiree* is not rooted in current reality but in a previous life stage, retirement creates a void in a retiree's Identity, which will be filled by another Identity, based on who they choose to be and live in retirement (or what they do and grow into as a result). Their ex-Profession may still be a part of their Identity to the extent they still identity with that phase of their life, but it's no longer a Facet of Life they engage in. Accordingly, it cannot continue to actively Feed their Identity.

It is often said that when you retire from work you "retire into something else." This is an insightful statement, but very few realize how much depth there is to it. The *retiring into* is not simply replacing activities related to work with other activities. Instead, it's a transitioning into a new Identity as retirees unwind and disconnect from their Profession and assume another meaningful Identity over time, through a process of "Becoming." It is more accurate to say you "retire into *someone* else," which eventually happens. When retirees complete the transition in their Identity, their Profession, which once may have been an essential Identity Component, will simply offer sentimental memories as part of their life experiences. How long this transition will take depends on how intimately they had identified with their work and how quickly they will be able to engage meaningfully in a Facet of Life that will Feed into a new Identity. The more important an ex-Identity was, the larger the void and the greater need for a new Identity[1] to become part of them.

Retirees may still view their Profession as an important part of who they are. Hopefully, everyone who is retired holds fond memories of work, whether due to the importance of their work assignments, or relationships with co-workers and the individuals they served. This is certainly true for those who felt highly accomplished in their work and received resounding recognition. The more they felt adored and validated through their work, the harder it may be for them to move on from their Identity in their Profession, and the greater the danger is that they live in the past. It is not uncommon for retirees to go back to work. Sometimes the financial compensation is an important part of their decision, but in many cases there's another overarching reason: they have not established a new Identity that is fulfilling, and they are trying to connect with what was fulfilling before they retired. It may take time for an ex-Identity to be shed entirely. You know an ex-Identity has been completely replaced when looking back at it, there is minimal if any regret that it is no longer part of who you are, and you would not "trade places."

Unwinding an obsolete Identity or winding up a new one happens over time based on Facet of Life activities retirees engage in. The more they engage in Facets of Life, the more the Facets grow in importance to the point of the retiree Becoming a new Identity.[2] Conversely, by neglecting to engage in an Identity through activities related to it, the Identity will fade. Using our example of golf, Becoming an avid golfer would entail playing it frequently, practicing regularly to improve a swing, investing money on lessons and on quality equipment, and socializing and connecting with other golfers-...as the importance of golf commands an increasingly greater portion of conscious and subconscious thoughts and actions. In time, "golfer" will develop into an Identity and continue to grow in importance the more the golfer Feeds it.

> Ask yourself, "Who is it that you are interested in Becoming?"

On the contrary, someone who was an avid golfer and is no longer able to play might still watch it on TV, read publications, maintain contact with golfing friends, and continue to identify as a golfer. Eventually, their interest may wane, and as they distance themselves from this part of their Identity, golf will eventually be fairly irrelevant to them and no longer a part of who they see themselves as being. Let's apply this principle to our Identity in Retirement.

UNWINDING & WINDING UP IDENTITIES

Figure 8a

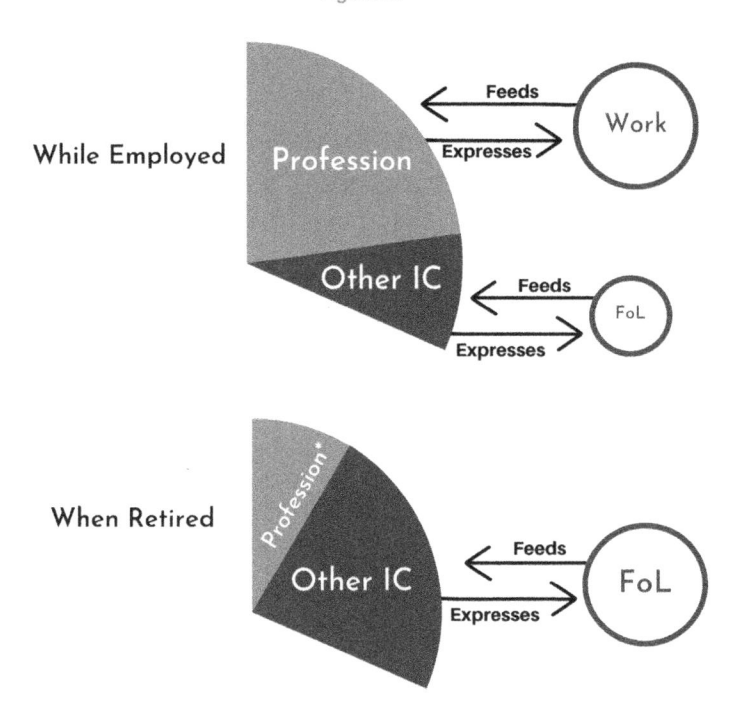

While Employed

Profession — Feeds/Expresses — Work

Other IC — Feeds/Expresses — FoL

When Retired

Profession* / Other IC — Feeds/Expresses — FoL

IC = Identity Component
FoL = Facet of Life
 * Even though a retiree is no longer employed, Profession can still be an Identity component if it has not been fully replaced, but no Facet of Life is attached to it.

A retiree's emotional connection with Work may have been limited and it might not have been a significant part of their lives, but merely a Descriptor of what they did for a living. They may have had a meaningful Identity in Facets of Life other than their Work while they were employed, and they may not need to pursue a new Identity to feel fulfilled. In retirement, they can use their unlimited discretionary time to immerse themselves in Facets of Life they enjoyed while they were working to Feed the Identity connected to it, or search for another. Unwinding any minimal Identity they may have had in their Profession will not be challenging.

If you identified with your work and are "moving on" in retirement by engaging with any of the many things life has to offer, you *will* assume a new Identity as activities related to Work stop. This new Identity might or might not be fulfilling. Depending on whether you apply a Realizement Perspective to your retirement, the Facets of Life you engage in will determine if you are strategically creating the Identity you want for yourself or coincidentally being shaped by what you wind up doing repeatedly and allow to become part of your life. Because we tend to make choices with little thought or reflection, this process is rarely intentional, resulting in us participating in haphazard activities. Retirees may be surprised to find out down the road that what they devoted themselves to grew into Becoming their Chief Identity.

Retirees who have a traditional Retirement mindset, often develop a pleasure focus and channel their unlimited discretionary time to Recreation Facet of Life activities. They enjoy meeting new people and exploring new outlets for "fun and games." Over time, what appears to be unrelated recreational lifestyle activities; turn out not to be disassociated but bound together as Recreation Facet of Life activities. Doing "whatever

BECOMING A RECREATIONIST

Figure 8b

Seeming disconnected recreational activities...

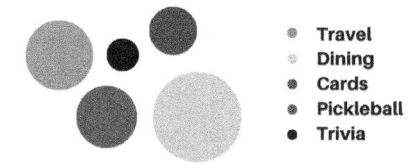

- Travel
- Dining
- Cards
- Pickleball
- Trivia

..are connected through Recreationist Identity Component.

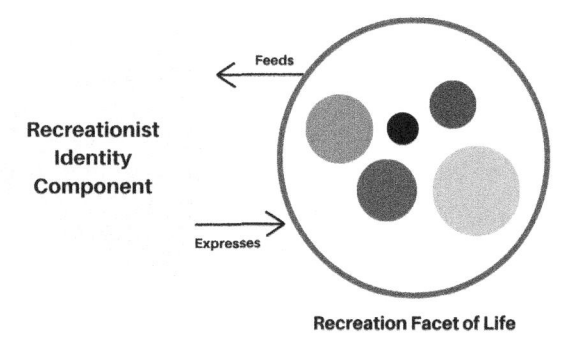

Recreationist Identity Component

Feeds
Expresses

Recreation Facet of Life

they want, whenever they want" can result in them Becoming retirees with a Recreationist Identity. This simply was not possible when they had work and family responsibilities. Now that they have unlimited discretionary time, there's the option to Feed this Facet of Life.

Facet of Life	Feeds	Identity Component
Recreation	→	Recreationist (retired)

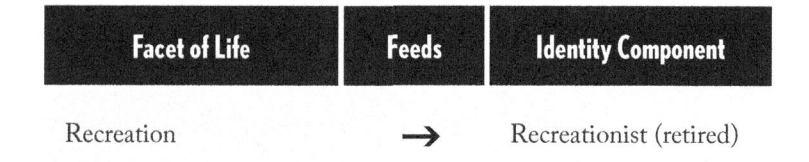

Work activities that used to Feed a Profession Identity can be replaced by recreation activities that now Feed a Recreationist Identity, as the former Identity gets wound down and is replaced by winding up the new Recreationist Identity. Let's unfold this process of transformation.

A recreation lifestyle is inconsistent with the strong work ethic we had over the course of 30+ years marked by work demands and family sacrifices. In order for a recreation lifestyle to become an Identity, it demands a transformation of our Beliefs/Values/Character to permit ourselves a "life of leisure,"[3] particularly if it becomes a Chief Identity. This potential 180-degree change requires that our values shift to permit, prefer, prioritize, then pursue Recreation Facets of Life as our hopeful source of fulfillment. Because the activities aren't naturally fulfilling, there's an increasing need for more and regular stimulation to maintain emotional pleasure that provides a sense of satisfaction but is unable to provide deeper fulfillment. Sooner or later, retirees may conclude that their bountiful social activities are making them busier than ever, but their recreational lifestyle of "the more, the better" is not providing them with the satisfaction they are looking for-... and perhaps they look for employment. Retirees often fail to realize the reason their lives may be less than fulfilling is not because the activities themselves are inadequate, but because their new recreation activities are not meaningful or what may be their new Recreationist Chief Identity is not providing the fulfillment they had hoped for.

The Realizement Perspective takes a deeper, more strategic approach for spending time — doing what matters most in your life. When the Facets of Life you choose to do for fun are expressions of your Identity and not Descriptors disconnected from who you are (but in time could become a new Identity), you can experience both enjoyment and fulfillment. Intentionally opting for Facets of Life that reinforce the most important parts of your Identity you want to develop is instrumental for Becoming who you want. As long as you maintain a growth mentality, Realizement is a continual process of self-discovery and growth.

Retirees who adopt the Realizement Perspective for this stage in life do not see recreation as an end onto itself but a means to an end. In the list of Facets of Life discussion in the previous chapter, "Recreation" was described as both "participating in pleasurable activities-…because of the enjoyment," and providing "stimulation and refreshment." Unlimited enjoyment of pleasurable activities can be exhausting, but "stimulation and refreshment" are always helpful for purposeful living, directing energies where they are most productive. Recreation can also uncover specific interests you may want to explore and maybe develop into a new Identity Component, separate from a Recreationist Identity.

The process of building into an Identity Component starts with considering which ones resonate with who you want to be and how they line up with your Beliefs/Values/Character. Ask yourself who it is that you are interested in Becoming during

AVOCATION IDENTITY COMPONENT
Figure 8c

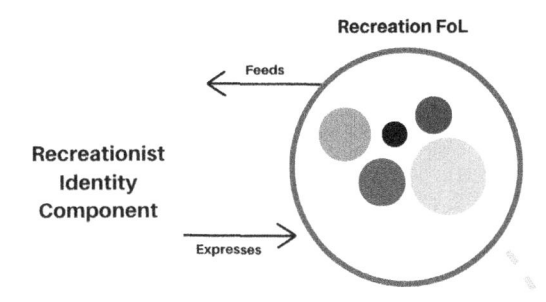

Important element of Recreation Facet of Life becomes a separate Hobby Facet of Life feeding the Avocation Identity Component.

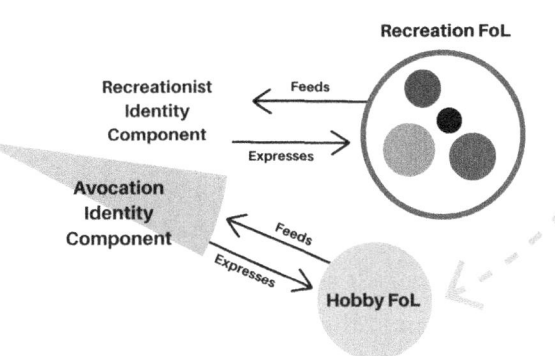

this stage of your life when you definitely will be changing.[4] Once you have an Identity Component in mind, participate in Facet of Life activities that will promote your growth into that part of who you want to be. Slowly, the activities will increase in importance beyond Descriptor actions as you invest your efforts pursuing a Facet of Life that Feeds a new Identity Component. The process of Becoming may take trying new things or rediscovering parts of yourself that were important to you earlier in your life, as you determine which Identity Components are worthy of being part of you that you would like to have as your own. It may also require that you shed Identity Components that no longer suit your evolving vision of who you are Becoming, which means you should not Feed them anymore. The Identity Components that you give most priority to will begin to drive your deepest desires, control more of your thoughts, and be the focus of your actions.[5] They will occupy the majority of your "mental space"[6] and be what your unlimited discretionary time gets allocated to. Retirement is a critical time to reflect on who you want to be and dedicate yourself to Feeding meaningful Identity Components you build into a fulfilling Chief Identify, part of your Complete Identity.

You have a fulfilling Identity when is it is connected to what matters most in life to you. It allows you to feel good about who you are and helps you experience contentment. With it, you do not struggle with insecurity and have nothing you need to prove to others or to your worst critic — yourself — so you can accept and love yourself as you are. You can be completely honest with yourself and others and be vulnerable about your strengths and your limitations. Having a meaningful Identity does not mean that you are not actively seeking more from life around you or from your own life; you just don't have the need to accomplish anything or struggle searching for something to fill a void in your life, because you already feel whole. Success does provide joy and satisfaction from the efforts you committed yourself to, but what you do is not tied to your view of who you are and doing is not necessary for feeling better about yourself. The best way to know you have a fulfilling Identity is when it is lived out in a Life Purpose you find fulfilling.

Creating a fulfilling Identity is important not just because it meets this Core Soul Need, but because it is foundational to a life path that will meet your Life Purpose (Core Soul Need). A fulfilling Life Purpose will affirm a fulfilling Identity when you make a difference in the world around you, that is important to you.

Endnotes

1   If whatever your Identity was wrapped up in is no longer true of you, you may experience a deep sense of loss. You may feel like "nobody" in your own eyes, until you gain another Identity. Retirees who are no longer working in their Profession but still identify with it are maintaining their emotional connection to some extent with what they view as a highlight of their life. However, by clinging to an Identity from a previous stage of life, they are unable to move past what is now an obsolete Identity — but perhaps still relevant to them. An ex-Identity that doesn't reflect life as they know it may seem better than no Identity or whatever alternative Identities, they are able to claim at the time. (This helps explain why celebrities and sports figures repeatedly come "out of retirement" to seek comebacks.) In their attempt to bridge the gap between their current reality and their desire to relive their previous Identity, they may medicate with self-destructive behaviors and addictions that sadly become a significant part of their Complete Identity. This creates an even wider gap between who they see themselves now relative to the highlight of their life. "Living in the past" is an indication that your Identity is not fulfilling and could be downright dangerous.

2   Just like anything in life, an Identity will increase and decrease in importance based on activity or inactivity. There is an escalating relationship between an Identity and its corresponding Facets of Life reflected by the amount of interest to pursue it: the more prominent an Identity Component is, the more interest there is to pursue it through a Facet of Life activity; and the more a Facet of Life is engaged in, the more it Feeds the Identity, which in turn generates more interest in pursuing Facets of Life that reinforce it. The opposite is true when there is less interest in an Identity, resulting in inactivity.

3   "Lifetime of leisure" is one of the retirement lifestyles retirees may select for themselves, along with such options as adventure, socialization, and family. However, a lifestyle is not the same thing as quality of life. As you settle into your lifestyle, be aware of how you view more important quality of life considerations, which is the true measure of the value of your life to you. (See endnote 1 in Chapter 12: Life Goals, Hopes, and Dreams.)

4   You may need to grow as a person of better character for an Identity you want to pursue to be true of you, since it must be supported by your Beliefs/Values/Character. Otherwise, what you do will just be a Descriptor. For example, if you want a meaningful Roles (Identity) of a volunteer, it requires you to have the Beliefs/Values/Character of concern and compassion for others in need for your engagement to be a heartfelt expression of who you are. Otherwise, volunteering will just be a Descriptor of something you check off your list so you can feel better about yourself.

5   Facet of Life actions Feed an Identity. They can grow in importance to you, even Becoming your Chief Identity that your deepest desires are attached to it. It will influence what you think about, and greatly affect what you do. Once it is set, it is hard to re-order the relative importance of your Identity Components and topple/replace "the Chief."

6   "Mental space" is where you do most of your life. Your thoughts are where you weigh options, feel emotions, test what you want to say, and project how you think things you do will turn out. What you choose to say and do is largely the result of the life you have been doing in your head.

Questions for Reflection

- What is your definition of a retiree? Do you have more of a traditional retirement or a Realizement Perspective related to this stage in life? How does that affect your view of yourself as a retiree?

- If your Profession was a meaningful part of your Identity, to what extent do you feel you are missing an important part of your life after you retired? In what ways have you not "moved on" from your Profession? Which Identity Component(s) are you trying to build into to replace your Profession Identity?

- How has your Identity changed since you retired? How is it sufficiently meaningful for you and in what ways is it lacking? (If you are not yet retired, how will your Identity need to change in retirement or it to be sufficiently meaningful to you?) In which of your Identity Components would it be important for you to grow, while Becoming who you want?

- Which Facets of Life are you primarily engaging in? How effective are they in Feeding a meaningful and fulfilling Identity? Which activities might you be interested in trying or pressing into to grow into an Identify that would be important for you?

- Do you view recreation primarily as pleasurable activities or also as a way to be refreshed and rejuvenated? To what extent might you have become a Recreationist? How do you feel about that? How might it be helpful to approach recreation more from an Realizement Perspective than a traditional retirement perspective?

9 Life Purpose

Life Purpose is the meaningful connection between your unique Identity and the world around you by what you do that is fulfilling to you and makes a difference for others. It's the reason you're on this earth and how you make the world a better place. As one of the Core Soul Needs, you must experience purposefulness in your life to feel satisfied and fulfilled at your innermost being. The more you engage with your surrounding community that is an important part of who you are, the more likely you will be to experience a meaningful Life Purpose.

Life Purpose is born out from your Chief Identity and is supported by many of your other Identity Categories, all focusing on what it is you want to do with your life that matters. Let's use as an example that, as part of your Beliefs/Values/Character, you are compassionate toward others in need. You find out about a local soup kitchen and decide to become a volunteer, which is a Descriptor of what you are doing with your time that you find enjoyable. As you volunteer more hours and develop relationships with the other volunteers and the clients who visit the kitchen, "volunteer" becomes less of a Descriptor and more an Identity

Component. It is no longer something you do but has become part of who you are as you have internalized it. You become more passionate about it, prioritizing your time and directing your attention toward it.

This may be something you really want to do and in fact, you may feel this is what you need to be doing at this stage of your life. Your Becoming a Volunteer may culminate in you elevating it as your Chief Identity, which would involve several Identity Components through the Life Purpose you are living out: Avocation (a chef who does the cooking), Faith (however you identify yourself spiritually who tries to help others meet their own spiritual needs), and a Community member (of the soup kitchen family connected with other volunteers, staff and clients, and also of your 55+ retirement community who recruits fellow residents, thereby connecting your communities). All these Identity Components are clustered around your Chief Identity as a Volunteer, closely tied to your Beliefs/Values/Character of compassion. The Life Purpose of volunteering that you are living out reinforces your Identity as a Volunteer by helping thousands of hungry people, providing deep fulfillment you will treasure for years to come.

> In some ways, we have as much of a need to make an impact as those we impact have a need for us to make it.

NEW CHIEF IDENTITY COMPONENT
Figure 9

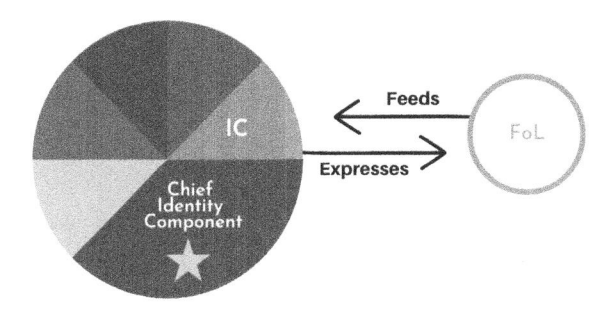

As a Chief Identity Component is not being lived out, another Identity Component that is Fed with great commitment becomes the new Chief Identity Component. The Facet of Life corresponding to it becomes a Life Purpose that is Lived Out and Reinforces the new Chief Identity.

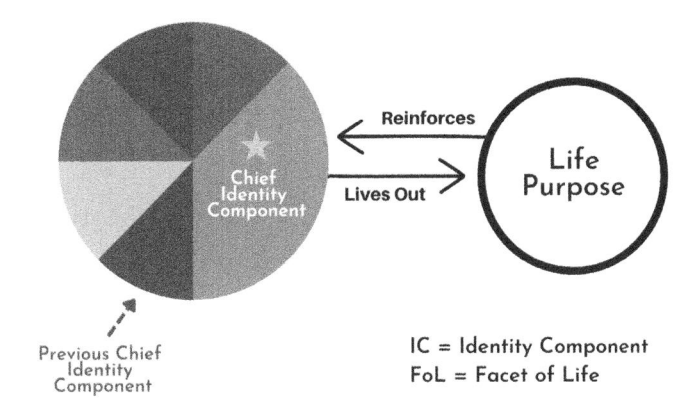

IC = Identity Component
FoL = Facet of Life

Sometimes life circumstances fall ideally into place, making your Life Purpose obvious: you are excited about and perhaps sense a burden for meeting the needs of others that you are perfectly and uniquely gifted for, and all the details about how you can make a difference line up. In other instances, circumstances don't line up in a way that may be as obvious. The opportunity presenting itself could fill an internal longing that reflects your personality and triggers your passion — something you *want* to do. Or you may have an intuition that there is a job for you to do. You sense an external leading (also known as a "calling")[1] that it is part of a plan for life — something you *have* to do, which could stem from your Spirituality if this is part of who you are. Whether the sense you have about the purpose for your life is an internal desire or an external leading — or a combination of both — is less relevant than living it out and experiencing the meaning and fulfillment you might be looking for.

For many folks, the concept of "Life Purpose" is abstract. They may have gone through life simply doing what was needed,[2] whether raising and providing for their family through their work or getting involved in a cause they believed in. Their family and work as well as the causes they took part in that were highly meaningful and fulfilling should probably be viewed as their Life Purpose at that time, but they may never have recognized their devoted efforts fulfilled their "life calling" at that stage in their lives. Not appreciating what you did as something you were called to do does not invalidate its value and importance or diminish the satisfaction you received in return. Almost without exception, people find energizing purposefulness in what they dedicate themselves to — regardless of whether it is recognized as a Life Purpose or not. And although we might not feel that our lot in life that we poured our efforts into was what we would have chosen, we are rewarded by a sense of accomplishment, nonetheless, having dutifully completed the tasks set before us.[3]

When people have worked in a Profession, they may have sensed to be their "calling" — or they at least found purposefulness in the work they devoted themselves to maybe for decades — they may unwittingly be disengaging from their Life Purpose when they retire. And because people typically retire when they are empty nesters and no longer have the responsibility of children to care and provide for, the two most important Life Purposes that retirees once had to meet their Core Soul Needs — family and work — are absent.[4] The importance of having this deep-rooted Life Purpose (Core Soul Need) met by living a life of significance does not change in retirement. We have unlimited discretionary time to do whatever we want and value and are not committed to fulfilling a specific Life Purpose. This provides an ideal situation to discover a passion for our lives that stems from our Chief Identity that will provide us with meaning beyond simply enjoying life. We need to be thoughtful about considering what we want our Life Purpose to be at this stage in life and decide how much discretionary time to devote to this part of our life.

In the spirit of enjoying life, retirees having a traditional Retirement Perspective start their new stage of life discovering what their long-awaited flexibility and freedom could look like. They try different experiences and develop new habits and patterns of life, and the pursuit of pleasure becomes a larger part of their lives than it had been for years. Over time, a focus on fun can create an Identity of a full-time Recreationist and if this is their Chief Identity it will also be their Life Purpose, meaning enjoyment is the main reason they exist. However, "fulfillment" is a word of expansiveness, conveying importance in what we do and realizing the potential of what lies ahead, ready for us to take on. There is a disconnect between the pursuit of pleasure which by nature is temporary and self-focused, and Life Purpose which is significant and directed at others. A determined pursuit of pleasure does not allow us to extend our Identity beyond our own existence to make the world a better place and experience fulfillment outside of the small space we occupy. The severe limitation of both the value and impact of recreation leaves Recreationists feeling empty and unfulfilled because it fails to meet their Core Soul Needs.

By expanding your significance beyond your existence and what just you alone can experience with your senses, you create a substantial opportunity to influence and make a difference in the world. A Realizement Perspective connects your Complete Identity with a receptive world that embraces who you are and what you can offer. In some ways, we have as much of a need to make an impact as those we impact have a need for us to make it. This is why an essential criterion for Life Purpose to be meaningful; is it must make a difference in the lives of others. You know your life is fulfilling if you would feel something important is missing, and the world would be at a loss; should you stop what you're doing. Conversely, you can know your life has minimal impact if you were to pass and the world around you would be no worse off. The drive to make a difference should be two-fold: to make a positive impact on others who would benefit from our efforts and experience the enjoyment and fulfillment resulting from the difference we made. The impact you are making and the satisfaction you are receiving as a result are your clues that you have a meaningful Life Purpose.

Retirement should be enjoyable, and retirees should look for outlets for recreation. They should not feel guilty about living the life the way they want — having fun and enjoying the fruits of their many years of labor. At the same time, retirees often find themselves busier in this stage of life than when they were working. This could be because they are doing what they feel they need to (perhaps related to family responsibilities with grandchildren) and/or spending their time chasing after what they think will bring enough pleasure to feel satisfied. What is not needed or even helpful for a fulfilling Life Purpose is "more" but "new" — a *new, fulfilling* Life Purpose tied to a meaningful Identity and not more pleasurable activities pursuing a Recreation Life Purpose that is unable to provide fulfillment. This starts with determining what Identity would be fulfilling and living it out intentionally. When you have discovered what that Identity is for you, limit those things from your calendar that do not have the potential to be fulfilling, especially if they are not particularly pleasurable. Feed the Identity you are Becoming with Facet of Life activities that support your vision for you who you want to be with an eye on how that would translate to a Life Purpose you can get excited about.

Pursuing your Life Purpose does not result in a loss of your Identity but provides an avenue to live out who you are in a meaningful way, contributing to the world around you. Your Life Purpose reinforces you Identity. The more closely your Life Purpose ties your Identity to something meaningful outside of yourself, the more fulfilling it is in your own life. Just like the richer view of Realization includes fulfillment and not solely consuming pleasure, Life Purpose is richer when connected to more than yourself. You experience deeper satisfaction when you "love your neighbor as yourself,"[5] connecting you to greater meaning than your pleasure. Exchanging some excess pleasure focused on yourself with what benefits others, we will experience "it is better to give than receive"[6] through fulfillment of our need for a meaningful Life Purpose.

Your Life Purpose need not be a grandiose requirement of your life (but it could be if it is your calling). You can experience purposeful living simply by interacting casually (yet purposefully) in your corner of the world by making a difference in the lives of people you encounter every day. But if you have the ambition to take on what you see as a larger role in life — and maybe even fulfill your "destiny" — your Life Purpose might require a greater commitment. Your focus on your Life Purpose will depend on how important it is for you to feel fulfilled and how satisfying your Life Purpose experiences are, tempered by the reality not having as many years left or the stamina and strength you once had. Your Life Purpose can also be the source of many of your pleasurable activities, although it may take more effort and determination. (More on this in Chapter 12: Life Goals, Hopes, and Dreams.) Your dedication to this Core Soul Need is a personal choice based on how instrumental you see your Life Purpose is to you and how much time you are able to commit to it given your other objectives in life and any other limitations you may have.

When you seek meaningfulness in addition to enjoyment as a retiree (or in any stage in life), be strategic about how you spend your most precious resources — your time. Be selective about which Facets of Life you engage in because of the Identity they will Feed and the Life Purpose that will result. As you reap the rewards of working for decades to enjoy your unlimited discretionary time, keep your Life Purpose at the forefront of your mind. This is what offers the most meaning to your pleasurable retirement lifestyle and serves as a guide for how to spend your time enjoying life. As you enjoy life while making a positive impact on the world around you, you can meet your Love (Core Soul Need) by deepening your connection with the people who support and share your Life Purpose and the people in whose lives you are making a difference.

Endnotes

1   Whereas the concept of an internal longing is easy to understand, the concept of an external calling is mysterious. Whether there is a plan for our lives that we may get a glimpse of and are drawn to follow, or if it is an attempt to legitimize our own internal desires is up to readers to assess for themselves, based on their own life experiences, and perhaps spiritual views.

2   Dutiful fulfillment of an obligation is an honorable Life Purpose worthy of acknowledgement and appreciation, regardless of the

magnitude of the impact — both in its significance to the beneficiaries and in the number of individuals who were impacted by it.

3   We cannot choose the circumstance we face but we can choose our response. Sometimes our results do not seem to reflect the effort we exerted. Regardless, we should be proud of our efforts and the results we were able to achieve without regard for the Life Purpose and what others may have achieved. Many of the opportunities before us and the circumstances needed to achieve what we may want are outside of our control.

4   One of the criteria for delaying retirement is to make sure the responsibilities we faced while we were employed are behind us. This frees us to enjoy our retirement and pursue the "want to's" without having to be concerned about the "have to's." These responsibilities may include financial considerations such as paying off the mortgage or car loans, paying off children's college loans and covering their wedding expenses. It can also include completing things that are important to us, such as an important project at work and waiting until the children are settled.

5   The second part of the Golden Rule found in the Gospel of Mark 12:30-31 is familiar to many. Loving others as much as you love yourself is an active, not a passive command. It's not simply refraining from causing harm but sacrificially bestowing kindness and blessings onto others. It stems from the first part of the Golden Rule — to love God with your entire being (heart, soul, mind, and strength) — which recognizes that sacrificial living benefiting others is empowered by being rooted in faith, dedication, and love for God. Readers must make their own connection between faith and an others-oriented purposefulness in life.

6   This adage is Biblically based (book of Acts 20:35), underscoring how the blessing of having given to others provides an even larger blessing to the giver.

Questions for Reflection

- What was your Life Purpose in various stages of your life? How was your Life Purpose tied to your occupation when you were working?

- What is your Life Purpose in this stage of your life? Is it sufficiently meaningful? What might you want it to be in the future?

- How is the Life Purpose you now have related to your Identity? Are any of your Identity Components prompting you to pursue a (different) Life Purpose?

- If you are searching for a Life Purpose, are you considering both an internal longing and external leading? What would you really like to do with your life that you would enjoy and allow you to make an impact? What might you feel you should do, taking into account your abilities and limitations given the place you are in at this time in your life?

- Are pleasure and enjoyment interfering with you experiencing meaning and fulfillment in your retirement or are they energizing and refreshing you to pursue your Life Purpose with more vigor?

10 Love

Life as we know it, generally revolves around ease and convenience. We do what is fast and easy, and gets the job done. This is true of all aspects of our lives, including how we seek pleasure and even who we choose to be in relationship with. We meet people in many ways: through familial relationships, by way of introduction, because of paths crossing, and sometimes through deliberate efforts, thinking certain people will add meaning to our lives. How relationships start is less relevant than how significant they are in our lives, which is why we choose to continue in them; or not. The priority we place on relationships determines the depth of the bond. Expedient Relationships are maintained due to convenience. However, if we invest in them, the emotional engagement can grow them into Enduring Relationships built on intentionality.

Expedient Relationships are practical and useful for helping us get what we need,[1] whether that is to accomplish tasks or meet our important need for socialization. They revolve around a consumer mentality, providing us with pleasure or whatever

> The priority we place on relationships determines the depth of the bond.

benefit we might seek from them. Because we can get something out of them without exerting much effort, they are useful but not particularly reliable. Sometimes we may be "looking for something"[2] when considering whether to start a relationship. We are cordial to folks that don't fit the profile, but will only begin a relationship if we think we would find it sufficiently enjoyable or beneficial. When we think a relationship has potential to be valuable — although the connection may be somewhat shallow — it passes the first hurdle for the relationship to begin. However, both parties must feel they are "getting enough out of it" for it to continue. Once it stops providing the value expected or is no longer convenient enough, it falls apart. As a result, Expedient Relationships are somewhat disposable, unless they grow into significant relationships, becoming more meaningful as more energy is invested in them.

Regardless of how enjoyable or beneficial they are, Expedient Relationships will last only until the common points of automatic contact remain.[3] This helps explain why Expedient Relationships dissolve when folks retire, relocate, change their life habits, or shift their interests — and life paths longer cross effortlessly. Even long-term Expedient Relationships that have been loving and wonderfully enjoyable will die off when the "touch points" cease. When this happens, it will become evident the relationship was not as significant as it may have appeared. That is not to say these casual relationships are not enjoyable, beneficial, or meaningful while they last, but they are somewhat transient.

Enduring Relationships are more resilient because the intentional effort that goes into building them results in deeper connections. We have these with individuals we value for who they are and not because of what they can provide us. Unlike Expedient Relationships that focus on what we want to get, these relationships are characterized by wanting to give and expressing our care for each other. We are more interested in being *in* the relationship than what we can get *out* of it. Continuing or building them depends entirely on the satisfaction from giving and receiving resulting from the emotional connection, which is accentuated by a common concern for each other. We are intentional about dedicating our time and emotional energy, even when changes in life make it challenging.[4] Interestingly, even though Expedient Relationships are mostly about enjoyment, Enduring Relationships can be more enjoyable because the connection accentuates the pleasure we experience from activities we may do together.

Enduring Relationships have the effect of multiplying our elation by reliving it when we share it with our friends and loved ones. They also have the effect of dissipating sorrows and pain. When one is hurting, another comes alongside dividing the emotional struggle. When two are experiencing the same difficulty, mutual consoling helps replace pain with compassion and understanding. People don't just add "spice to life," they are part of the essence of life itself. It is antithetical to human existence to do life without meaningful interaction with others.

The most important difference between Expedient and Enduring Relationships is the depth of the emotional connection. Expedient Relationships involve fairly routine life activities, typically around Descriptors, while Enduring Relationships help meet our Core Soul Needs — and usually revolve around our Identity because of Beliefs/Values/Character we have in common. We grow to love these folks, thereby meeting that essential Core Soul Need and we may be Peace Partners in each other's lives as well. Of all the people we encounter in our lives, lifelong friends, and family members[5] are often those whom we are most deeply connected with and love the most, and with whom we can have an authentic relationship to "speak into" each other's lives.

We defined "maximizing your enjoyment" as doing the things you enjoy the most with those you love the most — not with those you *enjoy* the most, but those you *love* the most. Love is inseparably linked to the special people who are essential for us to experience meaningful life. The most memorable and precious moments in life are those we share with those we love. In fact, the things we do and the experiences we have in life often have the meaning they do largely because of the loving people we share them with. This is why our enjoyment is more pleasurable when sharing it with the people we love the most and why they are part of our richest experiences.

As much as "Love" is talked about in our culture, it is a poorly defined word in the English language. In contrast, the Greek language offers distinctive terms that convey the various shades of meaning in the word. The concept of "unconditional love" ("agape," in Greek) has been discussed extensively in popular media. This intense, selfless commitment of love requires supernatural strength to be lived out in all circumstances. It may be our intention to love our children unconditionally, but the amount of emotional energy required to sustain unconditional love in a one-sided relationship might be too draining even in an unbreakable parent/child relationship. A relationship based on unconditional love is something we probably wouldn't consider expending on a non-family member.

For Enduring Relationships with dear friends that are meaningful and make our retirement amazing, a better understanding of the quality of love is "phileo," another of the Greek words for love. It has an emotional connection that goes beyond a casual friendship and is formed by a sense of unity. It is a bond of genuine care and affection, overflowing with enjoyment and appreciation. It involves give-and-take where the needs of both are met with a spirit of patience and kindness without expectations, but not without any limits (as with unconditional "agape" love) — although they can be stretched. It is generous and not demanding, with faith and trust in each other that empowers relationships to withstand the strain of disappointments and misunderstandings that all meaningful relationships experience to some degree. By building into emotionally satisfying family relationships with your best attempt at unconditional, "agape" love and deep friendships with "phileo" love, you will meet your Love (Core Soul Need) and at the same time help those you love to meet *their* need.[6]

The most powerful and satisfying relationships exist when folks truly care for one another and choose to enmesh their lives so intimately that life would not have the same meaning if they were not sharing it. You can know a relationship is an Enduring Relationship rooted in Love and not an Expedient Relationship if you were to mourn a loss of part of who you are should the Enduring Relationship end. The folks we have an Enduring Relationship with are not just in our life, they are part of our life.[7]

Both Expedient and Enduring Relationships are important in retirement for sharing life and providing comradery for enjoyable activities. The more casual Expedient Relationships make you laugh and smile for as long as they last, without expecting more from them than the small effort you are willing to invest in them. They are important for socialization and recreation. However, it's important to be thoughtful about the amount of time and effort you commit to Expedient Relationships as the more surface-level benefit they over competes for the time you are able to give to Enduring Relationships. Enduring Relationship provide greater depth and are a more intensely enjoyable, but they take more effort, concern, giving, and emotional commitment. Given the time and effort they require, you only have capacity for a limited number of these deep relationships.

When the people with whom you are doing the things you enjoy the most are also the individuals you love the most, it adds a wonderful relational component to maximizing your enjoyment. You enjoy the activity and get pleasure from your loved one's enjoyment too. It's like enjoying enjoyment! In addition to your Enduring Relationships allowing you to maximize your enjoyment, they help you meet your Love (Core Soul Need) and may also help you meet your Peace (Core Soul Need).

Endnotes

1   We are not taking advantage of people by being in relationships which fills needs we have. Clearly, there is "something in it for us," otherwise there would be no point to be in a relationship with someone you have minimal connection with. The other party probably has the same view of the relationship and will stay in the relationship for as long as they feel there is "something in it" for them as well.

2   It is wise to be discerning when determining who we want to do life with. This requires we know ourselves well enough to recognize the type of people we want to be in a relationship with or not.

3   Automatic contact points include neighbors saying hello when they see each other or dropping in to pay a visit; having regular interaction with co-workers; seeing friends in church every Sunday; exercising with someone at the gym, etc. These interactions will cease when people change their life patterns, and relationships that center on them will not survive.

4   Enduring Relationships continue even when life circumstances change, and we no longer share automatic touch points. They endure because the emotional connection goes beyond the practical benefits we gain from the relationship. When our schedules overlapped or we lived in closer proximity to each other, it was much easier to stay connected, but now it requires we make a special effort to stay in touch. The reality is that changes in life reduce the frequency of face-to-face contact and interactions that are important for maintaining emotional closeness. Physical separation cannot help but chip away at the relationship over time.

5   It is because they share the same foundational Identity and have invested countless hours doing life together that Family members share

a built-in connection providing natural intimacy. It offers the potential for a deeply meaningful, lasting love. (At the same time, families can be a source of deep hurts and scars because damaging interactions of varying degrees that have not been resolved. I apologize if I stirred up pain.)

6   Everyone needs an exchange of love — both to express it and receive it. By loving others, it helps them meet their need to receive it, and by accepting their love, it helps meet their need to express it.

7   The feeling of loss of an Expedient Relationship built around pleasure would be mostly limited to the interruption of the enjoyable activity you did together. This can be replaced much more easily with another individual or another activity than a loss of an Enduring Relationship can be.

Questions for Reflection

- Who are the people you have Enduring Relationships with that you feel most loved by and free to express your love to? Which Facets of Life are truly enjoyable to both of you that you might want to do together? What can you do to further strengthen your relationship?

- Which of your Expedient Relationships would you want to be more meaningful? How can you intentionally build into them for the relationships to be Enduring? Conversely, which of your Expedient Relationships might you want to pull back from?

- Who are the special people in your life that you are not as close to emotionally as you once were that you would like to re-connect with? What can you do to rekindle the relationship?

11 Peace

After years of relational, professional, social, governmental, and self-imposed demands in seemingly every aspect of life, retirees are ready to bail on the stresses of life and experience Peace that may have been absent in their lives. Whether they have had to carry the burden of family struggles, endure a challenging workplace environment, care for ailing parents, or just deal with the ongoing complexities surrounding them, life has worn them down. Peace is essential for not only enjoying retirement but replenishing our soul.

Retirees are ready and eager to replace stress with pleasure, reducing — if not totally eliminating — the tension that marked their lives for years. Knowing that less hassles means more peace, retirees fill their schedules with enjoyable, hassle-free activities and social interaction. They insulate themselves with enjoyment and don't have time for whatever they don't want to be bothered by. Hopefully, any unavoidable frustration will be outweighed by the good things in life they are enjoying. Without a doubt, the sea of fun and games retirees submerge themselves in can be awesome, but it may also deceive them into thinking all is well, when, in reality, the Peace they desperately need may be missing from their recreation lifestyle. Retirees may be consciously or subconsciously surrounding themselves with busyness to escape from whatever it is in their life that is making authentic Peace elusive.

Peace is essential for personal wellness, but we seem to notice and value it more when it is missing. We might gain a better understanding of Peace by exploring some of its antonyms when we are not experiencing it in our circumstances, our relationships, and our inner being.[1] When things are "not right" in our circumstances or relationships, or when we internally feel out of sorts, "peace stealers" — upheaval, strife, and worry — can invade our restful wellbeing.

> Peace is not achieved, it's experienced.

The word "peace" can be appreciated at a deeper level by examining the Hebrew word "shalom" that communicates more than just the absence of peace stealers. The context of shalom includes a broader, fuller perspective than how we individually feel. It encompasses a multitude of individuals interconnected through family, society, ethnicity, and community, all striving toward a mutual goal to embrace tranquility, harmony, and wholeness. Shalom reflects the essence of deep, abundant life, integrating personal wellness with that of the larger whole, in all aspects of life, including safety, health, and justice. The beautiful, holistic nature of the word is easier to appreciate when we understand the root word shalom as "complete." When there is completeness, there is no need to strive to fill a void because nothing is lacking internally, although outside influences can try to disrupt and create an imbalance. In the Jewish culture, by wishing someone shalom when bidding farewell, they bestow their hope that the peace the individual goes out with is not disrupted, and their companion in life returns in peace. Comparing a lifestyle that focuses on seeking pleasure and avoiding stress to "shalom" exposes its inadequacy for providing comforting, fulfilling Peace. As a roadmap to experiencing Peace, simply pursuing pleasure may not get you to the true destination you are seeking.

Circumstances that surround us and the relationships we are in can promote an enjoyable life, liberty to do what we want, and the pursuit of happiness-…or detract from it. Naturally, people seek tranquility in their lives through "Circumstantial Peace" — by getting situations in our life and relationships in order. We figure if things around us are okay, then we're okay. The shortcoming of this strategy is it binds us to circumstances that we have limited ability to impact, and even in those instances that we can control our situations, our effectiveness is often limited. And when our efforts to remove sources of stress in our lives are successful, we don't necessarily experience Peace. When it comes to our relationships, we can try to manage them as well as we can, but we aren't able to control how people relate with us. Because we cannot change what is outside our control, relationships and unreliable circumstances can attack our Peace at any moment. Relationships may not be, and circumstances definitely are not reliable sources of the Peace we need at the core of our being.

Some folks equate peace with having their essential needs in life met, such as good health, meaningful relationships, and sufficient financial resources. Other folks feel that in addition to having their essential needs met, they must avoid and eliminate stress and frustration in as many areas of their life as they can. They may choose to fill their lives with recreation and pleasure but run the risk of creating a lifestyle where they need these activities to have Peace. Recreation doesn't eliminate or reduce problems of life and other than serving as a temporary distraction, it is neither the remedy nor does it provide the solace people need to deal with disruptions of Peace in their lives. As this strategy settles into being their routine, they begin to associate — then equate — Peace with pleasure. In time, they may require — if not demand — continual positive stimulation to avoid negativity and enjoy life.[2]

If we are not careful, we can develop an attitude of entitlement and steal our *own* Peace by becoming generally discontent, hard to please, quick to complain and slow to express appreciation. We may live like we need a checklist of things in life to "go our way" to experience Peace (and when even relatively minor things don't go according to plan, it triggers stress and frustration). This view of "peace" may be less related to the presence or absence of favorable circumstances and more of a struggle with contentment — requiring a lifestyle we feel we deserve and should control. Not only does this approach to pursuing Peace depend on circumstances only partly under our control, but we tend to redefine what we need to be at Peace. Such peace is subjective, unpredictable, and fleeting, and it cannot satisfy.

Fortunately, there is a something more powerful that determines whether we experience Peace in and through our surroundings. It's how we process both the favorable and unfavorable aspects of life and allow them to affect us. Searching for Peace *in the midst* of life events filled with chaos and conflict is a less effective strategy than experiencing Peace *regardless of* the events of life. The good news is we can control our reaction to our circumstances and determine to be at Peace and satisfy this Core Soul Need, regardless.

Whether we experience Peace or not is ultimately based on how we process circumstances. As helpful as favorable situations can be for you to feel at peace, your moment-by-moment outlook is more important than the specific circumstances of your life. If something is troubling you, you can seek to change it or choose for it not to bother you. Instead of grumbling something is not to your liking, you can be thankful about the good aspects related to it in the totality of the wonderful life around you.

We can experience Peace by solving problems and creating restful circumstances. When that fails, we can experience Peace in mildly troubling situations through various strategies we have developed, using "positive thinking," a combination of reasoning and hope that things will get better, reshuffling what we spend our time thinking about, distractions, denial, and intestinal fortitude to "fight through" the reality we face, looking past what something is to what we think it can be. These strategies are helpful to a degree — until we are powerless to do anything and what we face is too much for us to bear. We need a source of hope that is trustworthy and more powerful than our circumstances, or there will be times we simply do not have Peace. If you are a person who can be mentally tough and be at Peace in all your circumstances, then you may not be in need of anything now, but there may come a time when the circumstances in life are more than you can bear. Where will you turn for Peace then?

What we need to be experiencing continually is a "Transcending Peace" that overcomes circumstances that do not promote peace and does not allow our Peace to be taken away in unpeaceful conditions. We can experience Peace when we are facing debilitating life circumstances we are powerless to overcome or even soften, when our trust and confidence is in something greater than our circumstances. This provides us reassuring confidence that our circumstances can be reversed, but regardless, there will be a beneficial outcome no matter what happens. This soulful comfort showers us with Peace regardless of what our circumstances may be. Depending on the severity of the circumstances, we may turn to faith in a supernatural source of strength to turn our reaction to the tragedies we experience from fear, worry and doubt, to hope, joy, and belief, which open the door to Peace.

Inner peace is what people really want but incorrectly think is achieved by modifying or manipulating their environment or how they view harsh situations. They do not recognize that true Peace rests in our soul. Peace is not achieved, it is experienced. Living with this radical approach to Peace does not ignore the realities we face but transcends our circumstances and surpasses our understanding of why we may be experiencing Peace when strife around us attacks our very being.

How we can experience Peace in situations that are neither calm nor hopeful is highly personal. It certainly has

TRANSCENDING PEACE
Figure 11

Circumstances: Chaos, Order, Confusion
Relationships: Unity, Strife, Discord
Transcending Peace / *Inner Peace*

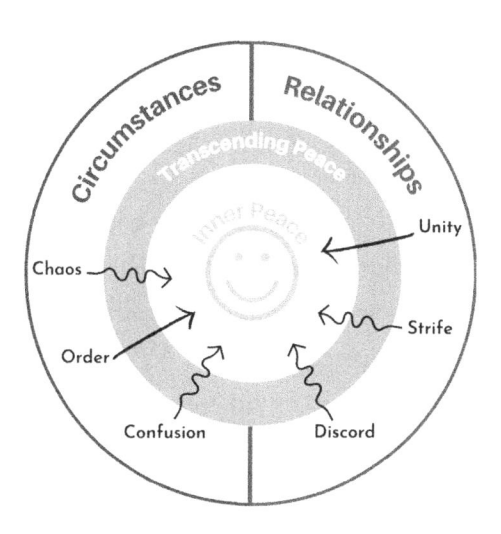

components of logic and emotion, as well as hope, faith, and perhaps philosophy and spirituality.[3] This is more than an issue of contentment or "looking at the bright side," but a radical change in a perspective on life that abounds with thankfulness "in everything" because you recognize you are not owed anything. It has a transforming influence in looking at circumstances not with just a twinge of hope that things will get better, but joyful[4] confidence that all things work out "for good," regardless of whether the outcome is what we would have chosen. This is not a theological discourse on religion, but an encouragement to consider whether faith has or should have a transcending influence on your life. Whatever strategy you use to experience Peace in the midst of turmoil,[5] make sure it will not fail you in the most difficult situations, when you need it most — those dreadful, tragic circumstances you are totally powerless to change, and you cannot ignore or deny their existence and consequences.

The Enduring relationships we are in are extraordinarily important to us, serving as channels through which we express and receive Love that meets this Core Soul Need. However, the individuals we have these relationships with can be even more connected to our lives by being Peace Partners[6] — showering us with emotional wellness in all situations and helping us meet our Peace (Core Soul Need). When these individuals or anyone we have contact with, speaks truth and assurance into our lives (as we can also do for them), they integrate hope with reality, and provide a safe place where we can feel rested and rejuvenated at our deepest level. In so doing, they will be dispensers of Peace in our lives.[7]

Your Core Soul Needs are intertwined — each one enabling the others to be experienced more effectively. Leveraging Peace when we feel our other Core Soul Needs are not being met can provide us with confidence and assurance to take the necessary steps to grow in those parts of our lives where we need to be fulfilled. Peace provides a greater capacity to love others and yourself, which is particularly important when you are struggling with a contentedness about who you are and what your Life Purpose is. Peace gives you space to consider what you need to think about and do to, providing clarity and Peace that ensues. When Peace is interconnected with Love, it strengthens you to ward off feelings of animosity and strife (peace stealers), making it easier for you to love those that are hard to which allows your Love you abound. On the flip side, when we are not experiencing Peace in our life, we can invite Peace into our inner being through the lens of our Core Soul Needs that are fulfilled — by reflecting on a fulfilling Identity and a satisfying Life Purpose that results from it, and the beautiful Love we share with others.

You are able to meet your Core Soul Needs of Identity, Life Purpose, Love, and Peace, thoroughly and experience amazing fulfillment with a Realizement Perspective in retirement by establishing and living your Life Goals, Hopes, and Dreams.

Endnotes

1   There are three areas where we want to experience Peace. Two are external: our circumstances (what is happening in the world around us) and our relationships (how we are interacting with others). The other is internal: our thoughts (how we are processing life), which ultimately is the only place Peace is experienced. Really, circumstances can be unrelated to Peace we are experiencing in our inner being.

2   Peace and enjoyment are two distinct categories of emotions. Having more of one doesn't increase nor does it lessen the other. Being super busy enjoying life may be an effective, temporary strategy to distract minds that are prone to worry or need a break from real stresses of life they are experiencing. The problem is enjoyment does not change circumstances nor provide any long-lasting peace (or more accurately, unawareness of peace stealers). Once the enjoyable activity is over and

it's "back to normal," it will almost be as if the enjoyment was never experienced.

3   Folks use different strategies to deal with troublesome situations, ranging from rational thinking (that our circumstances are really "not that bad"), to managing our reactions bodily (such as relaxing through slow breathing) to our emotions — perhaps ignoring them or overcoming them with "intestinal fortitude." Sometimes a philosophical tact may be helpful, thinking through circumstances and how we view them and why. Hope and faith are spiritual approaches to life circumstances, having a perspective that the material world is not the only world we are part of. None of these strategies change the circumstances we are powerless to effect, but they may provide us varying degrees of comfort, depending on our worldview.

4   The "Lord Is My Shepherd" 23rd Psalm speaks of a mindset of abundance — "my cup runneth over" (using the old King James Version translation) and recognizes the availability of a continual presence of goodness and mercy. By replacing optimistic or pessimistic variations of a scarcity perspective — whether our "glass half-full or half-empty" — with abundance, we can appreciate that we always have more blessings than we can contain.

5   The Christian faith taught and modeled by Jesus Christ takes the meaning of Peace to a transformational level. Jesus taught that the abiding, supernatural Transcending Peace he offers through faith is unlike the "Circumstantial Peace" the world offers. (Gospel of John 14:27) I am not qualified or able to offer a personal, informed opinion on what other faiths may offer.

6   Relationships may not start out with folks being Peace Partners in each other's lives, but through personal growth they can nurture each other as they develop into these roles. We should be intentionally building into those we have an Enduring Relationship with so we can grow into being Peace Partners for each other. Folks won't magically

fill a role without being taught or have it modeled for them. Part of our responsibility in having Peace Partners may entail us growing into Peace Partners ourselves that others may learn from us.

7   Be careful about the voices you are listening to. Just like you need to surround yourself with Peace Partners, you need to stay away from detractors in your life who can take you down an unhelpful path in your life journey. What you hear and believe can empower or discourage you from pushing ahead in the parts of life you need to make progress and have victory in. Otherwise, you can get stuck. Surround yourself with those who radiate positivity and truth.

Questions for Reflection

- How do you define Peace? How dependent are you on your circumstances to experience it?

- To what degree are you experiencing Peace now, and in what ways is it lacking? What are the negative factors or influences that are stealing your Peace? What can you change or do to eliminate them?

- In what ways do you find yourself staying busy enjoying life to escape the lack of Peace you are feeling? How has it been effective and ineffective? What can you do to gain real Peace in these parts of your life, instead of ignoring them and avoiding their effects?

- How do you experience Peace in unpeaceful situations? How do you overcome the lack of Circumstantial Peace in your life you cannot change? What is your source of power to do that? Do you see "Transcending Peace" as an option for your life when you are faced with dreadful circumstances that you are incapable of overcoming on your own? What does that look like for you?

- Do you have Peace Partners in your life who shower you with Peace in all your circumstances? Who are individuals you have an Enduring Relationship with that could grow into that role? Would anyone consider you as Peace Partner? How can you be more like that person or grow into that role?

12 Life Goals, Hopes, and Dreams

Life Goals, Hopes, and Dreams (LGHD) are the pinnacles of your life. They are the biggest "WOW" moments where maximizing your enjoyment during retirement doing the things you enjoy the most with those you love the most) intersects with experiencing amazing fulfillment (meeting all your Core Soul Needs). Living them is the culmination of the MaxAMAZING™ Your Retirement Life/Money System. You owe it to yourself to work through it, so your unlimited discretionary time and the assets you align with what is most important to you may help you realize your wonderful aspirations.

By definition, the Life Goals, Hopes, and Dreams you set for yourself will provide you with great enjoyment. They are the ecstatic realization of your ultimate desires. Experiencing them cannot help but provide the highest level of enjoyment. However, not all your LGHD will fulfill your Core Soul Needs. We'll look at two types, Enjoyment Life Goals, Hopes, and Dreams, and Fulfillment Life Goals, Hopes, and Dreams.

Enjoyment LGHD are a spectacular level of enjoyment you would like to experience that may have been something you have always wanted to do or a fairly recent desire you have set your mind on to live. Unlike maximizing your retirement, which is a lifestyle or experiences within your lifestyle, Enjoyment LGHD are discontinuous and break the norms of your life. You may have had these Enjoyment LGHD in mind for a while but were just unable to make plans to enjoy them until perhaps now that you are retired and have the time and financial means.[1] The awesome pleasure Enjoyment LGHD offer is fleeting, although they do offer some lasting value through the fond memories you will hold on to for the rest of your life. By living them out, you may have fulfilled a long-time dream, but they are not fulfilling per the Core Soul Needs framework. For example, you may finally have visited a destination you had always wanted to go to, and it may have provided you with the thrill you hoped it would-... and maybe you still get excited remembering it. It may have been an extraordinarily meaningful experience, but it is unlikely to have provided what you want and need most out of life if it is not tied to your Identity and therefore not a significant part of who you are.

Like Enjoyment LGHD, Fulfillment LGHD are enjoyable, but they are thoroughly meaningful and satisfying as well, tied to what matters most in your life. How truly important they are to you compared to the effort, the availability of resources necessary to achieve them, and whether deep down you really think they are possible, and you want to live them, will determine to what extent you will commit yourself to them.

The aim of the Life/Money System is to experience the highest levels of enjoyment *and* fulfillment in our lives, tapping into who we are and what really matters to us. Fulfillment

LGHD take much more effort than Enjoyment ones do and require thoughtful reflection about what we devote ourselves to. We're delighted when we engage in them, but we don't fully realize and appreciate the full benefit of the mental and emotional energy we exerted, until we see them come to fruition, at which time we fully experience the fulfillment they offer.

It is essential to have a balance of Enjoyment LGHD and Fulfillment LGHD in the Realizement stage in life when you have unlimited discretionary time to pursue them while Becoming the person you want. Fulfillment LGHD place us at the absolute peak of our quality of life, but due to the effort required and delay before we reap their full benefit — and because our "number of days" is more limited — we may need to limit the scope of what we pursue. LGHD of the Enjoyment variety may not be as deeply fulfilling, but do not require the same lengthy commitment, as they indulge us with bursts of joy and excitement in our post-employment lives.

> The biggest "WOW" moments are where maximizing enjoyments meets amazing fulfillment.

Fulfillment LGHD are everything you can think of that you would really, really enjoy doing in your retirement and would make your life as fulfilling as it can be. They can be categorized in three Life Goals, Hopes, and Dreams Apexes — life at its fullest:

- Experiences and Relationships
- Accomplishments
- Impact

The Identity Core Soul Need is closely tied to our Life Purpose that stems from it but also reinforces our Identify. The Love (Core Soul Need) facilitates Peace while Peace helps increase our capacity to Love. The Identity/Life Purpose and the Life/Peace combinations of Core Soul Needs are referred to as "Legs." They both must be established to build the Life Goals, Hopes, and Dreams Apexes. Let's explore how each of these LGHD Apexes can be brilliantly enjoyable and fulfilling — helping us meet our Core Soul Needs.

Experience and Relationship Apexes are lived out when we are doing what we enjoy the most (Experiences) with those we

FULFILLMENT LIFE GOALS, HOPES, AND DREAMS APEX

Figure 13a

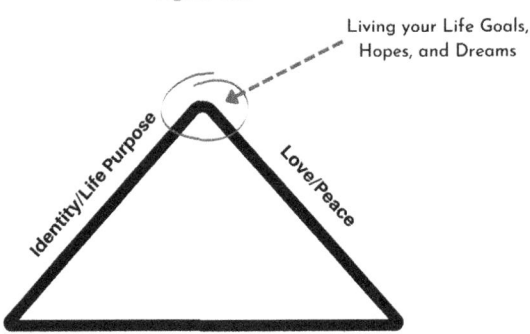

love the most (Relationships) in a way this is also meaningful to us. It is the definition of maximizing your enjoyment in retirement with the addition of providing fulfillment. "Experiences" and "Relationships" are grouped together because we invariably do the things that are most special to us with those who are most special to us, as the shared enjoyment is part of the experience itself.

We can enjoy life moment-by-moment — and even more so with those we love dearly — but we do not live at the top of the Experience and Relationship Apex (or any of the Apexes) continuously. Of course, you could be maximizing your enjoyment in retirement and absolutely loving everything about your retirement lifestyle in your ideal environment, and you might be thoroughly content and thankful as well. It could be said you are "living the dream" by how you simply do life every day when you retired. However, without discounting you may truly have a remarkable quality of life, the wonderful ongoing experiences and relationships you are enjoying would put you in the base of this Apex. Even if a lifestyle is enjoyable and offers fulfillment, we want to focus on an Apex being just that — an infrequent highpoint in your life and not a common, enjoyable occurrence. This requires spikes in enjoyment while your Core Soul Needs are being fulfilled.

Ascending to the top of the Experience and Relationship Apex where our Core Soul Needs of Love and Peace are met is largely determined by the quality and purposefulness of our interactions with others. As described in the Love and Peace chapters, quality interactions with people we do life with can promote Love and Peace. We need people in our lives who are both the source and object of our Love and help instill Peace in our lives. Typically, these are the folks we have Enduring Relationships with. If while we're "having a blast" we experience complete relational connectedness (Love) and an undiminished sense of wellbeing (Peace), we have scaled the Love/Peace Leg of this Apex.

Identity and Life Purpose are the Core Soul Needs that are more challenging for our Experiences and Relationships to fulfill. There is no shortage of opportunities to maximize our enjoyment in retirement through activities we can participate in with folks we can experience Love and Peace with, but they could be unrelated to who we are (Identity) and what we want our lives to count for (Life Purpose). For experiences and relationships to fulfill our LGHD, they must be connected to who we are: unique individuals who are passionate about what we want our lives to count for. By intentionally seeking great activities (Facets of Life) that reinforce our most important Identity Components, we craft a vision to scale the Identity/Life Purpose Leg of the Apex.

Accomplishment Apexes are realized when we achieve goals based on our Identity and Life Purpose that meet these Core Soul Needs. Accomplishment Apexes can be actualized in any of the Facets of Life that stem from our Chief (or a prominent) Identity. These Apexes may percolate in the back of our minds for a long time before we figure out how to pursue them — should we decide to commit to them. When we embark on this part of our life journey and progress toward achieving what we set out to do, the Life Purpose fueling our LGHD intertwines more closely with our Identity and reinforces it through the efforts we devote ourselves to, that are necessary for them to become reality. As the Identity becomes more pronounced, it is lived out more fully through our Life

Purpose. We experience a spiral effect of being more dedicated to our Life Purpose that is more fulfilling to us, reinforcing an Identity that becomes increasing more important to us, lived out through an increasingly more fulfilling Life Purpose-... When we achieve our Life Goals, Hopes, and Dreams, we cannot but revel in the Accomplishment.

Accomplishments unhitched from Love and Peace (Core Soul Needs) are self-focused (something *I* did-... usually with a sense of pride and perhaps some degree of gloating). Even if others may benefit, these accomplishments are generally done for our personal emotional benefit to feel good about who we are and what we have done. Recognition of our achievement from others might be important, and sometimes the recognition *is* the accomplishment.

As highly effective as accomplishments can be in helping us meet our need for Identity and Life Purpose, pursuing them without being mindful of all our Core Souls Needs may be detrimental. The more important the activities we engage in are to us and the more we dedicate ourselves to them, the more they impact our Identity — either reinforcing it or Feeding an Identity Component that will become increasingly important to us over time. We must be careful that our life pursuits are what we want for our lives both from the standpoint of where they will take us (is that the destination we really want for our lives?) and who we are Becoming in the process (will we like the new version of ourselves at least as much as our current one?).

Seeking accomplishments that hinder us from meeting our need for Love and Peace, can unravel our lives. These latter two Core Soul Needs can only be met when our achievements are focused on others or somehow connect us to the people we Love. The Love Core Soul Need is not promoted through self-focused Accomplishments by others admiring us for what we achieved.[2] Monumental Accomplishments demand excessive time and emotional energy, creating imbalance in our lives. The greater the commitment that is necessary for achieving them, the greater the stresses on other parts of our lives. This often results in the collateral damage of strained or fractured relationships with those we ironically say we love the most, as they compete with the goals we set for ourselves for the primary affection of our heart. We need to be certain to include the people we say we love the most in a way that is meaningful to *them* throughout our journey, so they share our elation and want to be with the person we have become when we arrive at our Accomplishment destination.

An effective strategy for ensuring that an accomplishment we set our minds and hearts on could be an Accomplishment Apex in line with our Core Soul Need of Love is to be certain the individual(s) we are joined with in life (a spouse or life partner and perhaps close family members and even indispensable friends) share our passion and commitment to that same goal, or at a minimum are supportive of it and are willing to make sacrifices in other parts of life we share. We cannot climb the Love/Peace Leg of the Accomplishment Apex by ourselves and need to continue building our Love relationships with those we journey or create new ones in the process. This will also help us be at Peace during the times we struggle to meet our goal, perhaps with the encouragement of those we love and are supporting us in our quest.

Our need for a satisfying Identity must have been met before we set out to meet an Accomplishment LGHD. When the Identity we want for ourselves depends on success, it will stand in the way of us experiencing Peace as we strive to accomplish our goals. Our actions must be an outflow of our currently fulfilling Identity who we already see ourselves as being, and not be necessary for us to accomplish something to prove who we can be after we achieve something that will define us. Otherwise, we will be experiencing a battle at the heart of who we are — the person we want to become thru our accomplishment or the person we are not content to be. If we don't accomplish our LGHD in this Apex, we would feel disappointed, but if the pursuit originated from an Identity and Life Purpose that we already experience fulfillment in and through, the accomplishment (or lack thereof) will not affect our view of who we are or the importance of our life. If an objective for our LGHD is to feel accomplished and thus meet our need for Identity, we will not experience Peace throughout the process, but only after we accomplish it and feel a burden was lifted by "arriving as person we want to be," and if we don't succeed, we may feel we failed as a person and question our very worth. It is essential to disconnect who we are from our success; our Identity will be conditional on what we accomplish and necessary for our self-acceptance.

There is a danger of "ratcheting up accomplishments" where achievements are never fully appreciated because success often breeds the need for additional success we must subsequently achieve to feel accomplished anew. The cycle can be endless, and we will not be content with success that is not truly fulfilling at our Core Soul Need level. This is particularly true of our Identity. Success will call for new milestones requiring additional sacrifice and ignite additional stress (lack of Peace).[3] The only peace [4] that is gained is the temporary relief from striving and worrying whether we might not be able to meet the next goal-… which lasts only as long as it takes to ramp up another goal. This is particularly common when the accomplishment is a financial objective — and especially when we compare ourselves financially with others. Grasping for "ratcheted up" accomplishments and goals based on financial comparisons can evade our attempt for experiencing Peace and should not be established as LGHD (Accomplishment Apex). They can never be counted on to satisfy because comparisons often are moving targets, and we are prone to replace our benchmarks with whatever else we may set our eyes on.[5]

The primary appeal of scaling this Apex is to give direction to a Life Purpose [6] through Facets of Life emanating from an existing fulfilling Identity. This provides a fulfilling Life Purpose both through the pursuit and the climactic elation when we accomplish our goal. Because the Identity/Life Purpose Leg is more evident in this Apex, we must be sure that we are concurrently progressing up the complementary Love/Peace Leg to stabilize the Apex, or it will "fall over." We must be careful that the Apex is not too ambitious given the resources available to us and how long we will stay committed to our goal, given our stage in life. This will ensure that we balance what it takes to succeed with the most important relationships in our lives, where we experience Love and Peace.

Impact Apexes are achieved when we make a difference we are excited about in our world, that has the stamp of our Identity and meets our Core Soul Needs. Impact Indexes are similar to Accomplishment Apexes, except the primary focus is the betterment of others and not our achievement of it. As is true of Accomplishments, the Impact we are trying to make stems from our Identity which spawns a Life Purpose. The difference is that in addition to involving Life Facets related to our Identity Category, an Impact Apex engages compassion in our Beliefs/Values/Character.[7] It is also more likely that the Life Purpose related to making an Impact may have more of an "external leading" element – something we feel we have to do — than the Accomplishment LGHD Apex, which would have the "internal longing" variety — something we have our heart set on and want to do.

We can be confident that an Impact Apex will help meet our Core Soul Needs for a meaningful Identity and Life Purpose because what we engage in is based on our Chief Identity, that is especially tightly knit with our Beliefs/Values/Character. While working to reach our Impact goals, we are both getting satisfaction from living our Life Purpose and reinforcing our Identity. Because giving of ourselves is highly personal, this Apex has the potential to create Enduring Relationships with those we labor to make an Impact, and positive emotional connection with those who benefit from of our selfless efforts. Both groups of individuals may help us meet our Love (Core Soul Need). We can — and should! — receive personal fulfillment from making a difference, but we need to be careful that our focus does not shift from selflessly helping others to meeting our emotional needs to feel accomplished by leaving our footprint on something we were involved in. If we are honest, the motivation behind making an Impact can be self-serving. We stand in danger of "using" those we are having a positive impact on to meet a goal to love ourselves and what we are accomplishing. A disingenuous motive would discredit our Identity as being compassionate givers of our time and/or money and invalidate our efforts to fulfill our Love (Core Soul Need), although we still might feel good about ourselves.[8]

The discussion related to experiencing Peace when pursing this Apex applies just as it did to the Accomplishment Apex: being fixated on the end goal can create stress, wondering if you will meet it. When your motivation is based on an existing, fulfilling Identity with nothing to prove to yourself, just knowing you are doing what you have a longing for or are "called to do" provides Peace. Simply being on the right track in life can take off the pressure from having to achieve an ultimate goal — especially if your limitations may prevent you from seeing it to completion. Besides, the idea of making an Impact is part of a journey you probably share with others who will add to your Impact when you eventually are unable to. With nothing to gain or lose in our view of who we are, whether we attain our goal or not does not impact who we are. This frees us to never fail at our deepest, Core Soul Need level. *That* is Peace!

If making an impact by giving of your financial resources is part of your Impact Apex, you are giving out of an "abundance" mindset where you are not worrying how the financial sacrifice impacts you. Your detachment from the money you are giving away to make a difference in people's lives provides Peace by separating you [9] from any need you may have for it or any benefit you could derive from it. And since you freed yourself from relying on it this releases you from any control it may have over you.

Of the three Life Goals, Hopes, and Dreams Apexes, Impact is more naturally structured to meet all our Core Soul Needs. As is true with Accomplishment Apexes, the Identity/Life Purpose Leg is closely aligned with this Apex, and like Experiences and Relationships Apexes, the Love/Peace Leg is easily set. When both Legs of the Impact Apex are established, we just need generous helpings of enjoyment from the activities we get involved to make an Impact to shoot to the top of this Apex. The ultimate combination of enjoyment and fulfilment that Impact Apexes offer helps explain why individuals often get more involved in volunteering their time after they are retired and have more discretionary time.

When considering your LGHD, it is also important to note two helpful perspectives:

- Be honest about your motivations behind the LGHD that you are pursuing to be sure they are providing you the enjoyment and satisfaction you are looking for. You want to be certain they can meet all your Core Soul Needs and are worthy of you prioritizing your time as well as the mental and emotional energy you will expend. If they require too much of you, the stress they create will take a toll on your Peace and defeat the objective of meeting all your Core Soul Needs.

- Balance Enjoyment LGHD, that provide incredible enjoyment, with the more ambitious Fulfillment LGHD, that vault your fulfillment to the top of the Apexes, as you meet your Core Soul Needs. The Enjoyment LGHD will skyrocket your enjoyment level in retirement to help keep you motivated and encouraged to keep plugging away toward your Fulfillment LGHD that you will eventually reap the utmost fulfillment and enjoyment from.

TURNING MAXIMIZING YOUR ENJOYMENT TO FULFILLMENT
Figure 13b

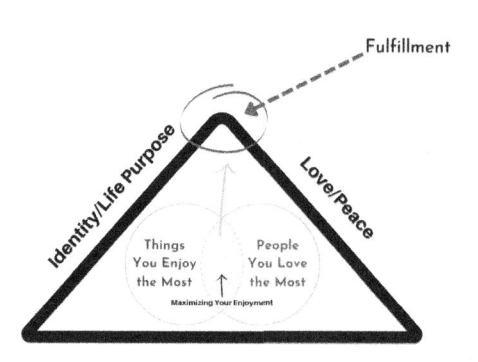

You can leverage the pleasure you enjoy from maximizing your retirement lifestyle to an Enjoyment LGHD by doing the same things you enjoy the most with those you love the most, but just in an extra-special way — perhaps by adding a spectacular experience to it. Using our example of being an avid golfer and assuming you are already playing with those you love the most, you could consider playing at a famous, exclusive golf course you may have dreamt of, or traveling to a fabulous part of the world you may have wanted to visit that has golf courses you would enjoy.

You can also modify what you are doing to maximize your enjoyment by pressing into a Facet of Life you are passionate about that stems from your Chief Identity. Elevate it to a Fulfillment LGHD, that would make a difference by benefiting others. It would be fulfilling and even more enjoyable for you by meeting your Core Soul Needs. Staying with our golf example, as your Life Purpose you could consider making an Impact by organizing a golf fundraiser for a charity you have a heart for that serves underprivileged children. It would stem from your Chief Identity of being concerned for those in need as part of your Beliefs/Values/Character, attaching your Identity as a golfer (Avocation) to how you live out who you are. To increase your connection with this part of your Identity and experience even more Love and Peace, through the organization you may be able to engage relationally with underprivileged children by introducing them to the game — personally instructing them, and maybe even funding their play. It will take more effort, but it will increase the enjoyment you get from golf in a new way by adding a Life Purpose and experiencing Love and Peace in the process. That could be an Impact "hole-in-one" for you.

With some thought and planning, the enjoyment and fulfillment you experience in retirement can be off-the charts, by taking those things you are already doing maximizing your enjoyment and making them superbly pleasurable Enjoyment LGHD, then turning them into Fulfillment LGHD by having them meet your Core Soul Needs. You will create an "Apex of Apexes."

If you are thinking about doing something important or special, plan and do it now. You will never be as healthy, energetic, and interested to do something you have been wanting to do as you are now, and the future is not guaranteed. We need to be intentional to realize our Life Goals, Hopes, and Dreams. This requires planning and may include funding. Otherwise, they just remain wishes.[10] The next step for making your LGHD a reality is to empower them by *Bringing Your Money to Life*™.

Endnotes

1   The difference between "maximizing your enjoyment" doing what you enjoy the most with those you love the most and "Enjoyment Life Goals Hopes, and Dreams" is how frequently they are experienced and their "wow" factor. Maximizing what you enjoy most with those you love the most describes events that occur more regularly and are part of your predictable lifestyle (which could be fabulous). Enjoyment Life Goals, Hopes, and Dreams are grander experiences that you experience less frequently. They would have to be uncommon to evoke a feeling of wonder or there would be nothing special to Hope or Dream we may experience one day.

2   Love is experienced though an exchange of giving and receiving — loving and being loved. Being admired by others is one-directional and somewhat shallow, without an opportunity for love to take root if it is not genuinely reciprocated. Seeking admiration is a form of self-love prompted by accomplishing something that is primarily important to us because of the praise we will receive as a result. Variations of narcissistic self-love cannot be emotionally fulfilling because fulfillment at the Core Soul Need level has a relational component that provide depth and lasting value, realized when our actions benefit others.

3   An ageless question about success is, "When is it enough?" Of course, there are many ways to answer this question, but they all use one of two standards — ourselves or others: success on our terms or success compared to or determined by others. The MaxAMAZING Your Retirement Life/Money System is interested in success as determined by your self-view of fulfillment. You have achieved enough success and do not *need* more only when you feel your Core Soul Need of Identity lived out through your Life Purpose has been fulfilled. This should not preclude you from chasing additional wins in your life; you just don't *need* them because you are complete and resultingly at Peace with yourself.

4   The word "peace" was not capitalized in this usage because it doesn't meet the Core Soul Need definition of Peace. A temporary, illusionary peace that lasts for only as long as the circumstances that support it, is not the fulfilling Peace anyone is looking for.

5   The opposite direction of comparing is also possible: instead of comparing ourselves "up" to push our own level of achievement, we might choose to compare "down" to others we stack up against favorably, to help us feel better about ourselves. Who we are and want to grow into Becoming should be our *only* standard for viewing ourselves. Comparing ourselves with others has unwanted side effects of developing an inadequate or inaccurate view of ourselves or invalidating others. Each of these outcomes can lead us to adopt an unhelpful and unhealthy slant on reality.

6   Having a fulfilling Identity does not automatically lead to a fulfilling Life Purpose. There must be purposeful activity. Impact LGHD (as well as Experiences and Relationships LGHD, and Accomplishment LGHD) uncover intentional actions tied to a meaningful Identity that might provide retirees with meaning they need in their lives. Sometimes what is necessary is just to know what to do.

7   If compassion is not an important part of your Beliefs/Values/Character, it will limit the type of activities you may choose to get involved in, but you could still make an important impact. You may be interested in an Accomplish LGHD that focuses more on the task than interacting with the individuals who would benefit from your kind generosity. If compassion is not an important aspect of your B/V/C composition, you may want to grow in this area to expand how you can make a greater difference in the world and in those you do life with and become more interested in doing so.

8   Similar to the discussion about Expedient Relationships, "using others" does not mean taking advantage of those we try to help, but gives us pause to consider the deep motivation of our heart. Is the wellbeing of others with "nothing in it for us" our genuine motivation for helping others, or do they primarily provide an opportunity for us to meet our own emotional need to feel important, valued, and appreciated? "Feeling good about yourself" is not a fulfilling exchange of Love and will not allow you to meet this Core Soul Need.

9   You will eventually be separated from your money — either when you are alive and give it away, or when you pass away and it instantaneously becomes part of your estate, waiting to be transferred to others.

10   Unlike Hopes and Dreams we would really like to see come to pass, wishes are whimsical afterthoughts made with little seriousness and at times, disconnected from reality. They are cast without any intention or perhaps interest in being realized. Hopes and Dreams, on the other hand, originate from who we are and what is important to us that we would love to live, but may never have sufficiently considered how they can come true.

Questions for Reflection

- Are your Life Goals, Hopes, and Dreams more for Enjoyment (which is not especially fulfilling) or Fulfillment (which is also enjoyable but takes more effort)? How could you modify the way you live your Enjoyment LGHD to meet your Core Soul Needs and make Enjoyment more fulfilling?

- What could you pursue to make your life absolutely spectacular? Which Apex would you classify them in — Experiences and Relationships, Accomplishments, or Impact? What might you consider for the other Apexes that would make your retirement as amazing as you want?

- How can you turn maximizing your enjoyment doing what enjoy most with the people you love the most into one of your Enjoyment LGHD by adding extraordinary enjoyment to it, or a Fulfillment LGHD by using it to meet your Core Soul Needs? How might you be able to integrate your Enjoyment and Fulfillment Life Goals, Hopes, and Dreams for the ultimate Apex of Apexes?

13 Bringing Your Money to Life™

There are two essential elements for living an enjoyable and fulfilling retirement: personal preparedness to meet your Core Souls Needs (Life Track) and financial planning to fund your physical needs, standard of living, [1] and whatever in life is most important to you that requires monetary resources (Money Track).

In Part 1, I laid out the Life Track to help you create a vision for what a Realizement Perspective could look like, showing how to maximize your enjoyment and experience amazing fulfillment by meeting your Core Soul Needs. This culminated in establishing your Life Goals, Hopes and Dreams. In Part 2, we will explore the Money Track and how to align your money with your Life Goals, Hopes, and Dreams (LGHD), Bringing Your Money to Life™.[2]

When we were earning money before retiring, we spent what was needed to pay our expenses and on extras we enjoyed. We set aside some as a reserve and invested the rest. When we retire, we no longer earn money and typically receive less income from "outside sources" (including Social Security, pensions, alimony, and trusts)[3] than when we were employed. The long-term objective we've had for our money for many years in anticipation of retirement has arrived. Our life's savings are now available to meet our needs for the rest of our life or whatever we choose to do with them. The wealth we have accumulated has three Destinations (where it will "wind up"): Spend as a supplement to our Social Security and other retirement income; Transfer to individuals while we are alive or when we pass; or continue to Accumulate it until we Spend it or Transfer it through our estate.[4]

> Align your money with whatever in life is most important to you!

We noted that all the truly incredible things we can do in life that would maximize our enjoyment and provide amazing fulfillment can be categorized in one of three Life Goals, Hopes, and Dreams (LGHD) Apexes: Experiences and Relationships, Accomplishments, and Impact. The three Destinations for our wealth align with the three LGHD Apexes: spending our wealth can fund wonderful Experiences with Relationships that we value highly; accumulating assets itself may be an Accomplishment we aspired to and could provide funding to Empower additional, related or alternative Accomplishment LGHD; and transferring wealth, to loved ones or causes we believe in, allows us to make an Impact that is meaningful and validates the effort of having built our wealth. By aligning the Financial Destination of your money with your LGHD Apex, you are Bringing Your Money to Life:

Financial Destination	Empower	Life Goals, Hopes, and Dreams
Spend	→	Experiences and Relationships
Accumulate	→	Accomplishments
Transfer	→	Impact

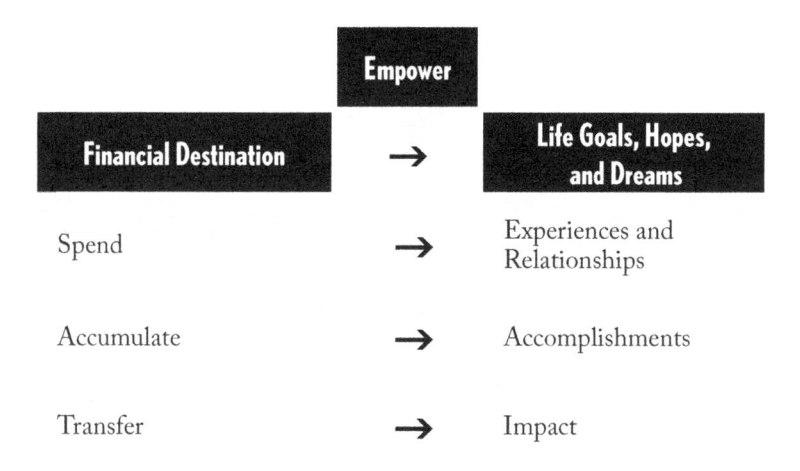

"Spend" is the Financial Destination for income received from outside sources and what our personal assets provide to pay for ongoing expenses or something that arises, whether planned or not. It is required to finance our necessities and discretionary purchases, to support our standard of living, and fund our experiences (what we want to do with those we want to do life with). Regular Spending is ongoing and is enabled by reoccurring income, while Sporadic Spending is infrequent and is supported by liquid reserves that provide a cushion to cover unusually high requirements for cash. We change our spending patterns over time, based on our preferences and the realities of life.

Now that you are retired, if between your outside sources of income and your accumulated wealth you can fund whatever you would like to do, you have accessibility to virtually "unlimited pleasure" in you unlimited discretionary time. When you structure your assets to pay for enjoyable and meaningful Experiences that allow you to engage however you want in the

Relationships that are important to you, they Empower you to live your Experiences and Relationships LGHD.

"Accumulate" is the Financial Destination of the growth of your wealth, whether from income you saved and invested, or what may have been Transferred to you (as a gift or an inheritance). The money you amassed provides a sense of Accomplishment of having accumulated it, and security and freedom from having wealth at your disposal. The financial strategy necessary for feeling financially successful had to have been started many years prior to retiring and might require continuing financial watchfulness for you to build your wealth or maintain its value.

Your Accumulated wealth serves as an intermediate Financial Destination for as long as you possess it – until you shift the focus of your Accomplishment from having attained wealth to using it to fund other Accomplishments you may value more highly than a larger account balance. Eventually, the wealth you Accumulate will find its way to one of two final Financial Destinations — you will either Spend it perhaps to fund Experiences and Relationships, or Transfer it to others while you are alive or upon your passing,[5] which could make a meaningful Impact. Any Financial Destination you select for your money can Empower your LGHD to the extent they can be acquired through your wealth.

"Transfer" is the Financial Destination for assets you did not spend that you want to be a Legacy for individuals and causes that reflect your Identity. You can do this sooner in the form of a gift while you are alive and can enjoy by seeing the Impact you are making, or later through your estate upon your passing. The recipients of gifts are typically bloodline (children, grandchildren, and perhaps great-grandchildren) but could include extended family members and friends especially if you have no descendants. Philanthropy is directed at causes and groups of individuals to whom you feel connected. The timing of a Transfer will depend on plans you might have (to Spend your money or your desire to hold on to it because of the importance it represents to you or the security it provides to pay for potential needs in the future, compared to the pleasure you experience when making a gift.

Passing through life, we gain wisdom and perhaps an appreciation for what our wealth can accomplish for others and not just for us. As we age, we may feel freer to part with a portion of our wealth that we are unlikely to need for ourselves — especially if the security and pride gained from possessing it becomes less important than the Impact we want it to have on others. The Transfer of your financial wealth to benefit others or make the world a better place can Empower you to meet your Impact LGHD that stem from your Values/Beliefs/Character. Effective financial and legal strategies can ensure the money you Transfer (Financial Destination) gets to the recipients for whom it was intended in the most expedient and tax-efficient manner.

How we go about aligning our money with the things in life that are most important to us will depend on the Approach we take to Allocate our assets to obtain the results we want from our money.

Endnotes

1   There are several terms that touch on the relationship between money and how we live: standard of living, lifestyle, and quality of life, in increasing order of relevance to our Core Soul Needs being met. Standard of living refers to the relationship between our financial resources and how we live. A higher standard of living requires more spending to pay for it and wealth to support it. Lifestyle refers to our choices related to the routines and rhythms of our life related to how we want to experience and interact with life surrounding us that may be constrained by what we can afford. Lifestyle has both financial and non-financial components, meaning some but not all aspects of the lifestyle require financial resources. Quality of Life is the value we ascribe to the beauty and fullness of our life. It is affected by our lifestyle, but more so how we view and do life. Finances are most important when maintaining a standard of living, or lifestyle. When focusing on our quality of life, finances are less important as we consider our Core Soul Needs. Finances are an important consideration related to a standard of living, decreasingly important for a lifestyle, and could be barely relevant for quality of life. Finances define the standard of living but could have no bearing on quality of life which is entirely determined by what we choose for it to be and what we want its meaningfulness to be to us.

2   The Bringing Your Money to Life process recognizes the real value of money lies in its potential to connect us with whatever it is in life that is important to us that is related to the economy. It is a technique that aligns or structures money consistent with our Values/Beliefs/Character to enhance our lives and make the life we envision possible.

3   These outside sources of income are listed in a decreasing order of likelihood of being owned by retirees or retirees being entitlement to receive payments from them. Another potential source of outside income

may be a type of income annuity, which has no account value and no option to receive additional distributions, similar to employer-sponsored pensions. When it is purchased by individuals, they trade an asset base with flexibility to take distributions are they desire for an income stream that has flexibility in how it is established, but afterward is virtually completely inflexible. These specific types of income annuity products are almost always acquired to provide income over the entire lifetime of an individual and perhaps also the spouse's. Privately owned income annuities are slightly less common than pensions, which are a type of annuity with lifetime income.

4   Net worth is an element of the Finances Identity Component that is important to some folks. In additional to the potential to be spent or transferred in the future, wealth provides a sense of Accomplishment and status to which some individuals attach their non-financial worth.

5   The accumulation of wealth is a topic of interesting, practical theological discussions. One is the concept of ownership. To whom does the money folks who take a "stewardship" view of money have in their possession belong to, and how free are they to use it as they wish? Is it theirs or does it belong to their Creator and Sustainer, and they just manage the wealth entrusted to them "on God's behalf" until they are separated from it when they physically die? Another is the purpose of wealth as expressed by King Solomon, renowned for his great wisdom. He describes the pursuit of acquiring wealth as pointless; we only have a short lifespan before we pass and will leave it to someone else. His advice is to enjoy and spend it.

Questions for Reflection

- How are your Financial Destinations Empowering your Life Goals, Hopes, and Dreams that they may be realized? How is your Spending allowing you to fund your Experiences and Relationships, how are your efforts in Accumulating providing you with Accomplishments you are looking for, and how will Transfer of your wealth allow you to make the Impact you would like?

- What are some ways you can Spend your money to meet your Experiences and Relationships LGHD more effectively?

- What Impact would you like to make with your assets — on whom, how and why? Would you prefer to experience the Impact and make a gift while you are alive or after you have passed?

- In what ways has your Accumulated wealth provided you fulfillment? Does the Importance of your wealth accrue to you more because of its dollar value or the potential practical use it offers for you to Spend it as needed (for things you enjoy or have to pay for) or Transfer it to others? Might your wealth be more valuable to you by providing you with more enjoyment and fulfillment from spending it on Experiences and Relationships LGHD or transferring it to realize Impact LGHD, rather than keeping it as accumulated wealth? What plans may you have for Spending or Transferring it while you are alive?

14 Investment Allocation Approach and Disposition Allocation Approach

Many pre-retirees make their decision to retire with much trepidation. They are looking forward to having the freedom to do what they want with their time, but their work provides them with steady income that meets their spending needs and allows them to continue putting money away. They have money set aside, but they're not comfortable they have enough to be able to afford to retire. As folks near the end of their career, they may be worried if their job will be secure until they are ready to retire on their terms.[1] The closer they approach retirement, the more reality sets in that their employment income will stop, and income will be reduced. Any shortages in retirement income will require them to make withdrawals from their nest egg. Their planning and preparation are no longer hypothetical as they finally take the financial plunge and decide to rely on their retirement income and life's savings.

A regular, predictable cash flow is foundational for being financially secure in our society. It is the starting point of financial planning. Without it, there can be no confidence in financial outcomes. When retirees stop working, they need to establish steady income between outside sources and their personal resources to pay for their necessities and fund the standard of living they want and can afford. From there, they should align their money with Financial Destinations that will Empower their Life Goals, Hopes, and Dreams.

The American workforce has become accustomed to an Investment Allocation Approach for retirement planning. Folks build their wealth hoping and maybe even expecting it will meet all the financial needs that arise when they are no longer earning income. As they approach retirement and eventually "pull the trigger," they may choose to reduce their investment risk to protect their wealth and be content with lower long-term growth (which becomes less meaningful the older they get).[2] Funding all their Regular and Sporadic Spending with outside income sources and taking distributions from Accumulated wealth as needed summarizes the financial planning behind this Approach.[3]

Regardless how effective they were in preparing and how they position their assets in retirement, there are four Financial Outputs that investment and financial instruments can provide:

- Income
- Growth
- Legacy
- Protection

Income is produced by vehicles that offer interest or pay dividends from profits. Growth is realized when an investment appreciates in value. A Legacy is provided when assets are transferred to others, and Protection is gained when individuals are insulated from the financial effects of unfortunate life circumstances that have a drastic economic impact, referred to as Bad Life Events. How we structure our assets to obtain the Financial Output we want will depend on our intentions for our assets and how predisposed we are to use our wealth... and the breadth of financial planning expertise at our disposal.

The Investment Allocation Approach used during employment, is a portfolio-based approach for meeting your financial needs throughout your retirement. You let your assets perform as they will and take distributions as needed. However, relying on an investment portfolio that you are still trying to grow — with perhaps less risk — might not be how you prefer to handle your finances in this stage in your life. It may have served you well, getting you to where you are financially, but what got you *to* retirement may not be the best strategy to get you *through* retirement. Continuing the same Approach you used throughout your working life — but may have recently modified to be less aggressive — might not be the only modification you should make to be certain your allocations will Empower your Life Goals, Hopes and Dreams. You may want your money to work smarter, not harder throughout your entire life for your Investment Allocation Approach to "work for you."[4]

> The approach that successfully got you to retirement, may not be the best one to get you THROUGH retirement.

A Disposition Allocation Approach has specific intended Destinations for how the Financial Output of your assets will be used. As a result, it utilizes a more direct and precise strategy for obtaining the Financial Output needed to meet both your living needs and Empower your Life Goals, Hopes, and Dreams. Unlike an Investment Allocation Approach where you don't know for sure how your assets will perform, with a Disposition Approach you decide exactly what you want your money to be used for and employ secure financial instruments with contractual provisions to achieve the specific task you purchased them for. The assets for which you do not have specific intentions are invested for Growth and distributed as needed — like the Investment Allocation Approach but only for this portion of your wealth.

Let's compare the Financial Output of both Approaches, noting how they direct your finances towards Financial Destinations to Empower your Life Goal, Hopes, and Dreams (LGHD).

Disposition Allocation Approach

Financial Output	Directed Toward	Financial Destination	Empower	Life Goals, Hopes, and Dreams
Income	→	Spend	→	Experiences and Relationships
Growth	→	Accumulate	→	Accomplishments
Legacy	→	Transfer	→	Impact
Protection	→	Secure	→	Assurance*

*Assurance is not a LGHD but provides Assurance that the LGHD will not be interrupted by Bad Life Events.

The Disposition Allocation Approach directly matches the Financial Output (Income, Growth, Legacy, or Protection) with the Financial Destination the assets are intended for (Spend, Accumulate, Transfer or Secure), based on our Disposition for how they will be used. This ensures assets will be in place to Empower our corresponding Life Goals, Hopes, and Dreams (Experiences and Relationships, Accomplishments, and Impact). Income annuities provide lifetime income for you to Spend on your Experiences and Relationships; Growth vehicles (perhaps with stipulated interest) allow you to Accumulate assets that foster a sense of Accomplishment; Legacy life insurance products provide a death benefit that is Transferred to those you want to have an Impact on upon your passing; and insurance products provide Protection to Secure your wealth so you can have Assurance that your wealth will be available to meet the Life Goals, Hopes, and Dreams (LGHD) that it was set up to Empower. (It should be noted that the ensuing Assurance from the Protection that insurance products provide is not one of our LGHD. Instead, being Secure is a defensive posture for Protecting the rest of our assets that are aligned to meet our LGHD. This also offers peace of mind that Bad Life Events won't prevent us from living our Dreams due to their potentially destructive financial consequences.)

> The Disposition Allocation Approach utilizes a direct strategy for obtaining the precise results you want from your assets.

Investment Allocation Approach

Financial Output	→	Directed Toward Financial Destination	→	Empower Life Goals, Hopes, and Dreams
Income	→	Spend	→	Experiences and Relationships
Growth	→	Accumulate	→	Accomplishments
~~Legacy~~ Growth	→	Accumulate ↳ Transfer	? →	Impact
~~Protection~~ Growth	→	Accumulate ↳ Secure	? →	Assurance*

*Assurance is not a LGHD but provides Assurance that the LGHD will not be interrupted by Bad Life Events.

Instead of using instruments that have a specifically defined Output, an Investment Allocation Approach relies on a diversified[5] portfolio of investments to produce Income and Growth to Spend and Growth to Accumulate. The Accumulated Growth can be used for any Financial Destination. The portfolio continues to Accumulate as an intermediate Destination, perhaps without specific intentions, until the owner decides to Spend it on Experiences and Relationships, use it to Empower an Accomplishment LGHD (possibly acquiring tangible assets the individual views as an Accomplishment to own), or Transfer it to make an Impact. In the meantime, it provides a Secure financial future, and the resulting Assurance that needs will be met as they arise. Because Growth is subject to uncertain performance and is subject to risk, it is an imprecise way to meet

ALLOCATION APPROACHES
Figure 14a

DISPOSITION

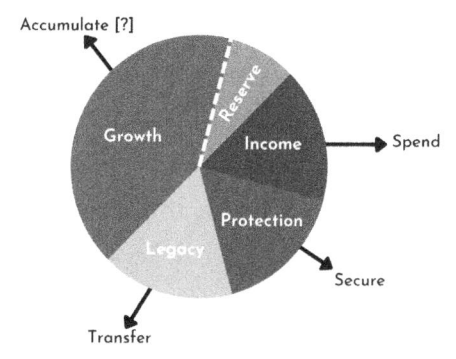

The certainty of the Financial Output in a Disposition Allocation Approach provides certainty for the Financial Destinations.

INVESTMENT

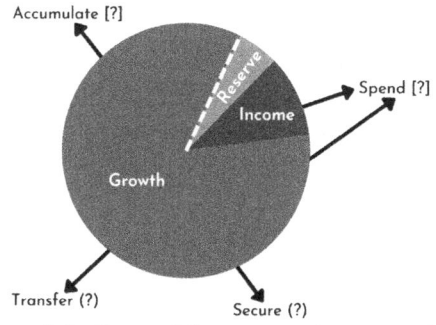

The uncertainty of the Financial Output in an Investment Allocation Approach provides uncertainty for the Financial Destinations.

the intentions retirees may have for their money. The portfolio must maintain sufficient value indefinitely for this Approach to be sustainable for as long as the retiree is alive. If the portfolio is depleted, it will no longer be able to meet any needs or leave a Legacy.

> The Investment Allocation Approach is portfolio-based, letting your assets perform as they will and take distributions as needed.

Both Approaches are susceptible to Bad Life Events, such as the death of a spouse that interrupts household income or catastrophic health expenses that result in crushing expenses. The difference is a Disposition Approach secures insurance coverage against them while an Investment Approach relies on wealth. An Investment Approach is also exposed to greater investment risk because the entire portfolio is invested. Whether due to Spending on a lifestyle and Experiences and Relationships, Transferring wealth, or paying for the effects of Bad Life Events, if retirees run out of money, they would be left with outside sources of income as their only financial resource to fund their standard of living.

Let's see how you may be able to use the two different Allocation Approaches to obtain the Financial Output needed to align your Financial Destinations with your Life Goals, Hopes, and Dreams (LGHD).

Income

Income is essential for supporting the Regular Spending for your basic living expenditures and the additional standard of living you enjoy as the fruits of your work life. The enjoyable and satisfying lifestyle it helps you create places you in the base of the Experiences and Relationship LGHD Apex. You also need resources to pay for Sporadic Spending on infrequent and irregular expenses, but more importantly to fund spectacular Experiences that shoot you to the top of the Apex. Some consumers [6] equate Income with simply taking distributions including perhaps Required Minimum Distributions from a portfolio, but investment income refers specifically to vehicles that generate cash flow that consumers can spend.

Consumers who use an Investment Allocation Approach to generate investment income almost always do this from an individual brokerage account, using holdings specifically selected for the Income they generate. The most common selections are dividend-paying stocks, bonds, limited partnerships, Real Estate Investment Trusts, and sometimes fixed growth annuities.[7] These various vehicles provide either stipulated or fluctuating payments with varying degrees of certainly. The intention of an income strategy is to select vehicles that generate cash flow interest, dividends, or profits to investors without requiring they invade the principal and cash out investment positions.

An Investment Allocation Approach often uses a "Pie-Chart Strategy," reflecting a retiree's risk tolerance. It is more concerned about the overall performance of holdings than considering income needs. Distributions are usually taken proportionately from the overall portfolio structured for Growth. It is the same strategy retirees used to build their wealth in preparation for retirement — the same account with largely the same holdings, but with a reduction in the percentage of equities to reduce risk.

A Timeline Investment Strategy is a more thoughtful technique for taking withdrawals from savings and investment accounts. It matches the liquidity, growth, and characteristics of financial instruments with when they are anticipated to be accessed, with the stipulation there is little to no risk they will have decreased in value at the time they are needed to be cashed out. Bank accounts and CDs are used for needs in the short-term (0-2 years), bonds and fixed growth annuities are used to meet needs in the medium-term (3-9 years), and allocations are made to equities for the long term (10+ years). On a regular basis, assets are shifted from the medium-term allocation to replenish money taken from the short-term holdings (that were withdrawn to meet the short-term needs), and in turn, long-term holdings are shifted to replenish the medium-term vehicles. This ensures funds are continually positioned to support reasonably expected spending needs over at least a ten-year period, without cashing out devalued investments that would be negatively impacted by unfavorable stock market performance. Assets that are not intended to be accessed for at least ten years are positioned for aggressive growth.

TIMELINE INVESTMENT STRATEGY
Figure 14b

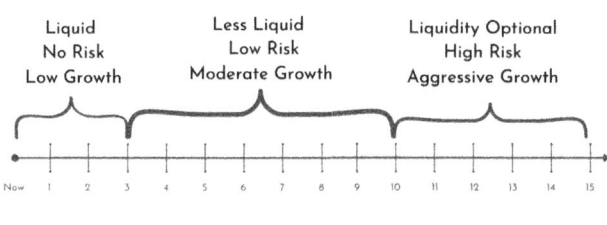

Liquid	Less Liquid	Liquidity Optional
No Risk	Low Risk	High Risk
Low Growth	Moderate Growth	Aggressive Growth

Number of Years

A Disposition Allocation Approach uses contractual lifetime payments from income annuities similar to pensions, to cover any shortfall in income necessary to meet your needs and fund your experiences. Income annuities are unique in that they are the only vehicles specifically designed to provide income for as long as the owner is alive (as well as the spouse, if that is how you choose to structure the payments). Folks who have a propensity to overspend might be particularly well-served by an income annuity that can help meet their income needs throughout their lives, no matter how long they live.

Growth

Obviously, Growth is directed toward the Accumulate Financial Destination. It is the top or perhaps even the only financial priority for an Investment Allocation Approach — building the wealth necessary to fund current and future need over the lifetime of the individual. It aligns with Accomplishment LGHD and may Empower other LGHD if wealth is sufficient. Growth will be effective for as long as wealth is sufficient to meet spending needs and fund LGHD. Growth is also important in a Disposition Allocation Approach for the portion of wealth without a specific intention for how it will be used and allocated to Accumulate.

Consumers are regularly presented with investment options touting their superior features. The "perfect" investment would have three characteristics that are important to consumers: safety, liquidity, and results (growth or income). However, there is no vehicle that can consistently provide all three. At best, you can have two of the three: safety and liquidity but poor results (bank instruments); liquidity and results but a lack of safety (stocks); and results and safety but limited liquidity (annuities).[8] Where bonds fit into this construct depends on the interest rate environment [9]. Every financial instrument has a structural defect that makes it risky, illiquid or a poor performer. You could try to improve a feature of a holding you do not like by making it safer, more liquid, or perform better, but you would have to give up something else in exchange: if you want more liquidity you will have to forego some safety or returns, if you want more performance you will have to give up some safety or liquidity, and if you want more safety, you must give up some returns or liquidity. You must determine the characteristics you require a vehicle to have and accept the one you don't like, but you can live with. Effective financial planning requires allocating these imperfect vehicles to obtain the "best results" given the amount of liquidity that is required and the safety that is desired.

NO PERFECT INVESTMENT
Figure 14c

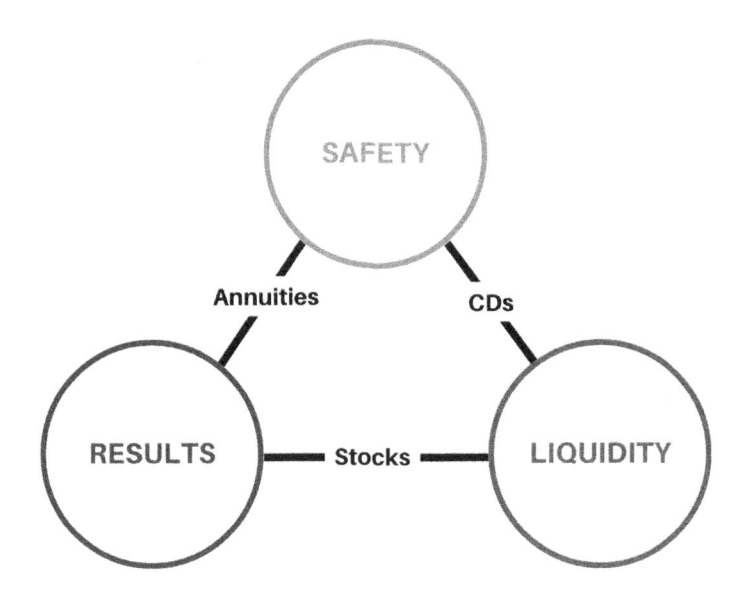

```
           SAFETY
         /        \
   Annuities      CDs
       /            \
  RESULTS —Stocks— LIQUIDITY
```

Both the Disposition and the Investment Allocation Approaches seek to build wealth with the appropriate level of risk. The biggest differences are adherents of a Disposition Approach tend to be more conservative in their investment holdings and may prefer vehicles that pay a fixed interest rate, such as CDs and short-term or multi-year guaranteed annuities. They are less interested in the "risky" stock market even if they don't plan to touch the money. If they have an investment account, it will often have a moderate risk allocation. It will typically have a larger percentage of bond holdings compared to those who prefer an Investment Allocation Approach and are more aggressive in their investment allocation as they seek higher growth.

A Reserve is the portion of a portfolio kept liquid in checking and savings accounts, short-term CD's, or a money market position in a brokerage account. It provides a cushion to cover Sporadic Spending for infrequent expenses and meet unexpected expenses as they arise-…and to fund Experiences and Relationships LGHD. It is also where excess income from outside sources and Required Minimum Distributions from IRAs may be held before they are spent or are reallocated to better growth options when the balance exceeds the need for liquidity. Disposition Allocation Approach consumers will typically have a larger cash Reserve, consistent with their conservative nature whereas Investment Allocation Approach folks will want to keep it to a minimum for higher productivity.

Legacy

Those for whom Impact is a LGHD Apex may choose to take the money they didn't spend on themselves and use it to make a difference in the lives of those they love or on a broader cross section of society or the world. Some folks aspire to have their children benefit from their assets and provide regular gifts or plan to leave them money upon their passing. Others look at the personal financial sacrifices they made over the years and prioritize their own enjoyment from the assets they were able to Accumulate. For those who do not have children, leaving an inheritance to family members who are not direct bloodline, friends, and charities is seldom a high priority.

A Disposition Allocation Approach is used by those who definitively want to leave money to others when they pass, by redirecting some of their income and assets to acquire a life insurance policy. This may provide them with more "freedom" to spend down assets, knowing that even if they should "spend their children's inheritance"[10] and eventually run out of money, they will at least leave a Legacy behind through the death benefit the policy will pay out.

An Investment Allocation Approach uses a strategy that Accumulates wealth as an intermediate Destination and Transfers "whatever is left" to heirs. It might not be a high priority of a retiree to leave a Legacy, but it does not necessarily convey a disinterest to make an Impact. Proponents of an Investment Allocation Approach could view building their estate by accumulating wealth and eliminating life insurance premiums as the most cost-effective way to achieve their Impact LGHD which would be true should they live "long enough."[11]

Unless you run out of money in your lifetime, the money you "can't take with you" will be left to whomever you choose. If you are confident you will not require a portion of your Accumulated wealth for Spending or for a Secure Financial

Destination to protect you from Bad Life Events, you may want to Transfer a portion of your assets as a Living Legacy before you pass away. This will allow you to enjoy the experience of your gift being received and provide you with an opportunity to speak into the lives of those receiving it to influence how they may use it, reflecting your Beliefs/Values/Character.

Security

Bad Life Events are the archenemies of Life Goals, Hopes, and Dreams on both the Life and Money Tracks of retirement preparedness. They disrupt our plans for our lives and can dismantle financial strategies put in place to support them. We rarely can prevent them, but we may be able to neutralize their consequences. Retirees have the option of trying to fund the ill effects of anticipated and unanticipated [12] catastrophic events using their own assets with an Investment Allocation Approach, or insuring themselves from their financial fallout through a Disposition Allocation Approach.

A Disposition Allocation Approach takes a defensive posture, obtaining insurance policies that produce Protection. It provides Assurance that should Bad Life Events occur, the resulting financial upheaval would be neutralized and not disrupt Life Goals, Hopes, and Dreams that still could be realized, as long as finances are Secure. By allocating some of your retirement income or a slice of your portfolio to cover the potential, destructive effects of perils, you can ensure the remainder of your portfolio will remains aligned with your LGHD Apexes, regardless of what occurs. It recognizes that previous investment results don't matter if all your wealth is used to pay for a nursing homes or home health care or depleted by a similarly financially catastrophic Bad Life Events.

An Investment Allocation Approach tends to ignore or underestimate the risk that Bad Life Events pose, or simply relies on wealth to cover the financial impact should they occur. This strategy is effective if the portfolio is truly sizable enough to withstand the financial consequences of the Bad Life Event by generating sufficient income or being liquidated as needed, and still being able to finance Life Goals, Hopes, and Dreams. Of particular concern is the scenario of a healthy retiree who has many enjoyable years to look forward to, but whose spouse incurs catastrophic healthcare costs that totally exhaust the family's financial resources. This would leave no assets for the healthy spouse to support their desired lifestyle or experience their LGHD. Without planning for risk and not having sufficient assets to self-fund it, both spouses are at risk should either suffer a cataclysmic health condition. Investment Allocation Approach adherents generally do not shy away from investment risk or risk in general, compared to those who prefer a more predictable Disposition route. Even if they do not have sufficient assets to self-fund debilitating Bad Life Events and they could afford to pay the premium for coverage, they may still reject insurance protection. By investing money instead of spending it on insurance premiums, they're opening themselves up to the possibility that the potential impact of the Events on their and their spouse's standard of living could be disastrous and could eliminate the prospect of leaving assets to loved ones.

Disposition and Investment Allocation Approaches are not exclusive and can be used interchangeably, although the mindset of these two Approaches is usually consistent across decisions related to all Financial Destinations. The overwhelming objective of those who prefer an Investment Allocation Approach is to build wealth, viewing a Disposition Approach as providing inferior results for wealth Accumulation. However, a Disposition Allocation Approach could help retirees who are cautious about investing [13] and keep a large Reserve in case it is needed to cover exceedingly large unanticipated expenses, get better financial outcomes. By securing insurance products that would cover the financial effect of Bad Life Events, they could free up some of the excessive liquid reserves they keep available for unintended expenses. This would allow them to redirect their funds to better-yielding instruments that have a little more risk or are less liquid. The result may be more favorable than what is essentially an Investment Allocation Approach using an asset base to prepare for Bad Life Events, but using vehicles that have little Growth Output.

Both Investment and Disposition Allocation Approaches have their strengths and weaknesses. The suitability of each depends on your financial circumstances and experience handling your money, your understanding and comfort with investment vehicles, income you receive from outside sources, your life expectancy, and how confident you are that your assets will perform the way you want. Those who are more knowledgeable about investing and are less concerned about investment risk will prefer an Investment Allocation Approach. While those who are less experienced and are interested in more certain financial outcomes may lean toward a Disposition Allocation Approach. Perhaps most importantly, your Approach will be heavily influenced by the financial planning strategies used by the financial advisors you trust to guide you in meeting your financial needs, based on their experience and expertise.[14]

Regardless of which Approach or combination of Approaches you implement, if your intentions for what your money will eventually be used for are important to you, be sure your allocations will result in your money winding up in the Financial Destinations you want. The MaxAMAZING™ Your Retirement Life/Money System is designed to help you recognize your Life Goals, Hopes, and Dreams based on what would make your retirement enjoyable and fulfilling. To the extent your wealth is necessary to fund what you want your life to look like, it is essential to align your wealth with whatever is most important to you. You want to be certain the Financial Output from your allocations will align your Financial Destinations with your Life Goal, Hopes, and Dreams to Empower and allow you to live them, and Bring Your Money to Life™!

Endnotes

1   When individuals are forced to leave their work and retire before they are ready, they have not made enough progress "winding down" the Identity they had in their profession and have not given enough consideration to which parts of their life they want to focus on. With a traditional retirement perspective, they don't know what they want

to do. With a more strategic Realizement Perspective, they have not decided who they are interested in Becoming, and which portions of their Identity they want to Feed with Facet of Life activities that will provide them with the enjoyment and fulfillment they want and need. Regardless of the retirement perspective, this leaves them unprepared to begin "winding up" other parts of their life and make the transition to this stage in their life.

2   The concept of "long-term" becomes increasingly less meaningful when you retire — and continue to age. The returns you receive in your portfolio are less important since the compounding effect (the greatest benefit of growth) is less powerful due to a shortened lifespan. Also, it is inadvisable to invest in vehicles that may lose value when you project you may need to access them because by doing so you would be realizing the loss. You may want to consider the potentially greater usefulness of your money early in retirement, and better able to take advantage of the opportunities to enjoy it instead of the "long-term" that is not as long for you as it once was.

3   An Investment Allocation Approach could be effective in meeting your needs throughout your life, but it would not be accurate to call it a "plan" from a financial planning perspective. At a minimum, a plan must have specific, measurable, and attainable goals coinciding with when you plan to need your financial resources. A comprehensive plan includes tax and estate planning. Certainly, folks can have all their financial needs met without optimizing their financial situation. Ultimately, the ones who benefit most from planning are often heirs. Some retirees don't see that as their concern, but it would stand to reason if they could do planning to benefit their heirs so they get more and the government gets less, why wouldn't they?

4   This is not a comment on the wisdom of using one approach or the other, but a recognition if a financial outcome relies on investment performance, the portfolio must perform for the financial objectives (that fund life objectives) to be obtained. With a Disposition Allocation

Approach, the financial instruments selected will get the job done that they were purchased for, but it will result in having less wealth as security and predictability are prioritized.

5   "Diversified" is a specific investment term that describes a portfolio designed with holdings expected to have *diverse* investment results in the *same* economic environment. In a certain economic situation, one investment will do relatively better than another (perhaps even increasing in value while the other decreases), and in subsequent periods the opposite may be true. The greater the disparity in the performance of two investments in the same period, the more diversified they are. In a truly diversified portfolio, there will always be holdings you are pleased with and others you are not. Consumers have adopted the term "diversified" to mean they own many different investments. However, if the performance of the various investments in a portfolio does not differ significantly over the course of a year, it is not diversified from a wealth management standpoint.

6   Consumers are referred to as individuals who seek to benefit from their assets without immersing themselves to understand the mechanics and underlying details of the performance of the instrument. Their interest in money is centered more on what money can achieve for them than how and why it is providing the results.

7   Annuities are a broad class of investments. Generally, they are used for growth or income. Growth annuities include variable annuities with investments in securities that have investment risk and charge investment fees and incur life insurance costs. Fixed growth annuities have either a declared rate or interest that is based on performance of the financial markets, but with no risk of loss and usually no fees. Income annuities are usually designed to provide income, usually over the lifetime of the owner (and perhaps a spouse). The features of annuities must match the financial objective of the consumer to be appropriate.

8   Annuities are a highly debated class of financial instruments. Some advisors tout them; and others shun them. Some consumers swear by

them, and others swear at them. The same can be said of stocks or any other financial vehicle. All financial instruments have advantages and disadvantages that make them appropriate or inappropriate for a specific consumer who has a specific objective in a specific situation. The appropriateness of a vehicle is not simply its characteristics but how its characteristics relate to the needs of a consumer. The fundamental dispute between financial products doesn't always center around the product's features, but which financial instruments advisors are licensed to sell. Different licenses are required to sell securities than to solicit insurance and annuity products. Most professionals are not licensed to sell both or for various reasons (including how well they understand it) prefer one to another, which creates a bias. Because consumers lack a proper understanding of financial instruments and implicitly trust the financial advisors they engage, financial advisors transfer their partiality to consumers. The most trustworthy advice is offered by financial advisors with a fiduciary obligation to place clients' interests above theirs, who provide a holistic approach to financial planning and are licensed to offer the full array of financial instruments available, which makes them unbiased in their recommendation. A consumer thinking about hiring a financial advisor should ask them what licenses they hold.

9   Bonds are debt instruments that pay a contractually stipulated interest rate for a set period, then return the amount that was borrowed. In normal market conditions they are safe (if they have a strong rating) and provide returns higher than CDs but lower than stocks. However, their value is related to the current interest environment relative to when they were issued. If they were issued at rates lower than current interest rates, they will be worth less because they are relatively unattractive compared to newly issued bonds that pay a higher interest rate. The opposite is true if they were issued with interest rates higher than current rates. If interest rates increase, the market value of bonds will decrease, and if they decrease, their market value will increase. The investment performance of bonds is a combination of the interest rate they earn

and the fluctuation in value based on changes in interest rates set by the Federal Reserve.

10   Inheritance may be associated with a sense of obligation on the part of a parent and entitlement for a child. The overwhelming objective of assets should be to meet the needs and to be enjoyed by their owners for as long as they are alive, as they hopefully Empower their Life Goals, Hopes, and Dreams. If there is a clear excess in assets, a Transfer while someone is alive through gifting can be a source of great enjoyment for both the giver and recipient. If there is an intention to absolutely provide assets upon passing, this would be a beneficial use of a permanent life insurance policy. The most important financial favor parents can provide their children is to remain financial independent for their entire lifetime, which means children will get "whatever is left," if there is anything left. Still, it is important to note that for some folks, providing financial resources to their children is what they most enjoy or want to do with their assets.

11   Speaking strictly about money, the proceeds from a life insurance policy are more valuable the sooner the insured individual passes. As time passes, the total premium paid into the policy increases and the face value is worth less due to inflation. The value of a death benefit compared to other investments must take into account the after-tax value each would provide. However, the longer an individual lives beyond life expectancy, the less relatively valuable the death benefit of an insurance policy would be relative to investment options which have stronger growth features.

12   Expected/unexpected describes whether we think something might happen or not. Anticipated/unanticipated refers to our heightened awareness that something we expect will happen, that could trigger us to take precaution. We face the possibility of experiencing many Bad Life Events — some expected and others not, with varying degrees of likelihood and financial consequences. For example, the likelihood of anyone passing away is certain. It is expected, but it may not be anticipated. Its financial impact depends on our overall financial

circumstances. However, whether care will be required in a nursing home is uncertain. If it is unexpected, it won't be anticipated, and it probably won't be planned for. As a result, this increases the potential negative impact it would have should it occur. How likely we view an event will happen, along with its timing and possible impact, will determine how motivated we may be to take preventive steps to neutralize its affect. If we fail to plan for an occurrence — regardless if we anticipate it or not — it can be devastating.

13   Referring to safe holdings that offer virtually no growth potential as "investments" is a misnomer. Investments have risk. Their anticipated return includes a premium on the investment — the additional return above the interest that vehicles with no risk pay — corresponding to the level of risk the investor is subject to. The greater the uncertainty of the return, the greater the premium it needs to offer in the form of a higher expected return. Placing funds in no- to low-risk vehicles that offer less growth than inflation will result in a loss of real purchasing power.

14   Whether consumers will use a Disposition Allocation in whole or in part is largely influenced by the advisors they work with. Advisors who work predominantly with securities will almost always exclusively offer an Investment Allocation Approach to their clients. Those who work primarily or solely with insurance products and annuities (and may not be licensed to sell or offer advice about securities), will center their practice on a Disposition Allocation Approach. Certainly, a combination of both provides more alternatives for meeting financial objectives.

Questions for Reflection

- What changes, if any, have you made to your portfolio since you retired? Have you reduced the investment risk you are exposed to, or changed to more of a "distribution and preservation" investment strategy?

- What do you see is the primary role of your portfolio for your financial future? How does your investment strategy support your overall financial strategy and the various objectives you may have, or is your investment strategy your financial strategy?

- Are you more conservative and pre-disposed to a Disposition Approach or more inclined to take an Investment Allocation Approach?

- How dependent is your financial future on the performance of your investment portfolio throughout your entire life? If you have not already, should you consider a Disposition Allocation Approach for your Spend, Transfer, or Protect Financial Destinations?

- Which of your Life Goals, Hopes, and Dreams could benefit from a Spend or Transfer Financial Destination instead of an Accumulate Destination?

- Which Bad Life Events could you take steps to protect yourself from to have the Assurance that they will not disrupt your Life Goals, Hopes, and Dreams?

15 It Was Nice to Spend Some Time Together

Thank you for taking time to peer into the accumulated wisdom I've gleaned from personal conversations with literally thousands of retirees. Throughout my rewarding 30+ year career in the financial service profession, it has been my honor to engage with wonderful folks who shared their life experiences with me and entrusted me to manage their life savings. I hope I have been at least somewhat successful in sharing these insights in a way that speaks into your life — challenging and encouraging you to take the necessary steps to get on a better life path that will lead you to the enjoyable and meaningful retirement you may be yearning for.

I'd like to offer you a few last words, some of which encapsulate concepts and strategies presented throughout the book, others to provide additional inspiration for you, and my offer to guide you further on your journey with additional resources that I am making available to you.

First, be who you are. No one is a version of you, and you are not a version of anyone else. You have grown into being who you are, and you will continue to grow into Becoming an even better version of yourself. Be comfortable being yourself. You have more imperfections and shortcomings than mastery. There is a whole lot more that you don't know, and you are not good at, than you know and have expertise in, as is true of everyone. That's reality. At the same time, there is nothing you need to prove to others, or yourself. Don't feel you need to impress others by who you are or pretending you are someone you are not but be comfortable in the package you are: a brilliantly integrated person. Like everyone, you have aspects that could be viewed as strong points or weak points (based on *someone's* standards), but regardless, they are all *your* points. As you go through life loving and being loved by others, love yourself and be loved by yourself.[1] See yourself as special and celebrate who you are.

Second, tear down barriers in your life that have stunted your personal growth — those requirements and expectations you and others have placed on you that you don't need to be part of your Identity or your Life Purpose. Give yourself permission to dream what your life can look like and what Experiences and Relationships, Accomplishments, and Impacts you want to live! One of my saddest observations in working with retirees who have poured their life into others, is somewhere along the way they gave up on their own Life Goals, Hopes, and Dreams. Sadder yet, they many have forgotten how to dream. Saddest of all, due to recurring disappointments, they have concluded that dreams are obsolete and no longer have a place in their lives. Change that. I'm not talking about simply

> Take the necessary steps to get on a better life path that will lead you to the retirement you may be yearning for.

having goals and plans, but with starry eyes (perhaps reminiscent of your wonder in childhood), let the "what if's" become Life Goals, Hopes, and Dreams that you turn into reality. Allow the Facets of Life you travel take you wherever your Identity wants to go. Dreaming is more than acceptable; it's indispensable for living the full retirement you want. It does require you reorient your mind, believing that much more is possible as you take the first step toward Becoming who you want and doing what you want. All this requires reflection and planning.

Third, surround yourself with the highest caliber people who have a genuine concern for you. Fullness of life abounds in the Love and Peace we experience when doing life with others. Higher quality people who share your beliefs and values and usher in a higher quality of life by making it both enjoyable and fulfilling. These are folks with whom you can be authentic and transparent because their heart's desire is to build you up, free from judgement. These folks can fill a Peace Partner role that emanates from the love you have for one other. Invite them to dream along with you and as you help each other discover your true Chief Identity. At the same time keep in mind they are on a journey, just like you, and have not mastered all they will one day and need grace from you just as much as you need it from them.

Next, be thoughtful and strategic about how you do life. Life is hard and planning is harder but what is harder yet is life without planning. This book explains the MaxAMAZING™ Your Retirement Life/Money System, specifically designed for you to take your retirement where you want, by adopting a Realizement Perspective. The companion digital workbook will guide you as you apply the principles to your retirement. You can access it at: MaxAMAZING.com

You are able to print the workbook or download it to complete it electronically. Do yourself the biggest favor you can and spend time with someone who would love to get to know you better-...yourself! As you work through the workbook, be honest and even vulnerable first with yourself then with whomever you do life with that you feel comfortable sharing with. This is particularly important as your think through your Identity — who you *really* are — and who you are interested in Becoming.

In addition to the workbook, the website contains various training resources about the MaxAMAZING Your Retirement Life/Money System that you can access without any cost or obligation. They will help you understand the System better and how to apply it to your life. A goal of this book and the resources is to lead you to is discovering your Life Goals, Hopes, and Dreams, which is the first huge step to MaxAMAZING Your Retirement, but the predominant goal is that you live them out. This may require you to align your assets with your Life Goals, Hope, and Dreams. The MaxAMAZING.com website has helpful financial resources to assist you, but for more resources also feel free to help yourself to the tools available on the website for my financial practice that will provide more assistance with Bringing Your Money to Life™. You can access this at: RetireeAdvisor.com.

Part of being strategic about life is being decisive. Both "yes" and "no" are important decision options. "I'll think about it" and "not now" often are diversions from making a "yes" or "no" decision you know you need to make. Many folks procrastinate making decisions and in so doing make passive decisions, meaning they indirectly decide not to do something by not specifically making a decision. Make active, purposeful decisions to either do something or not instead of "kicking the can down the road." Deciding through indecisiveness often results in not moving forward but continually looking back and wondering what you should do.

Last, get the professional assistance you need, from whomever you are comfortable with and is also qualified. This first includes counselors and life coaches to help you work through what you want your retirement to look like, which stems from your Identity then your Life Purpose, and leading to your Life Goals, Hopes and Dreams. From there, connect with a financial professional who can help make sure you align your finances to Empower them. Retirees who have prepared effectively for retirement may have done a good job building wealth to supplement their outside income sources and may have developed a strong understanding of investment strategies and effective investment skills. However, investing does not equal financial planning and investment skills do not automatically translate into comprehensive financial planning skills. Even traditional financial planning needs to go one step further, by aligning your money and the associated financial planning to optimize your financial results with your Life Goals, Hopes and Dreams. Wealth Accumulation and broader financial preparedness is not the same as preparedness for a Realizement approach to retirement.

When selecting a life coach, find someone you can relate to with whom you feel 100% free to open up to. Every worthwhile professional in their line of work is a highly engaged listener, able to both hear and feel what you are saying — carefully probing to help you discover things about you and your life that you may not have recognized. When selecting a financial advisor, look for the same qualities of a life coach — someone who "gets you" and accordingly understands what it is you want your money to achieve for you. Like a life coach leads you to personal self-discovery, a financial coach should lead you to financial self-discovery and help you understand the role money plays in your life. Just as importantly, the financial advisor should have expertise in her or his craft, advising how to Empower your Life Goals, Hopes, and Dreams through comprehensive financial planning. Your advisor should use the combination of Allocation Approaches (Investment or Disposition) that is most effective and comfortable for you.

Many retirees have achieved success in life and with finances, without the assistance of professional advice. At the same time there are life skills you may not have grasped and financial skills you may lack, that are necessary to achieve your objectives efficiently. Be honest with your limitations. Be open to involving counselors and financial advisors to help you grow in your personal life and free you from some of the responsibilities and details related to your financial affairs. No matter how successful you are, coaches can raise you to a higher level. This is true for world-class athletes, and it is true for how you do life and finances.

If you have a financial advisor[2] that you have been using, be sure you are prioritizing maximizing your financial results over your relationship. Too many times to count, I have encountered retirees who are guilty of what I call "misplaced loyalty"— elevating their loyalty to an advisor they have put a relationship ahead of the loyalty they have to themselves and their loved ones, which may be detrimental to their financial wellbeing. Don't settle for inferior financial outcomes because your advisor may not be skilled to provide fully integrated planning, or is limited to which financial instrument can be offered because how he or she is licensed, or may have become complacent about the services being provided assuming the personal relationship will retain your business. Be critical of what services and results you need from a financial advisor and 100% honest with yourself whether your advisor is delivering them. (Deep down inside, you know when you need to move on from your current advisor.) When looking for a financial advisor, you are wise to seek a fiduciary with a legal obligation to place your interest above their own.[3] At the same time, be sure you are acting as your *own* fiduciary and prioritizing your interest to optimize your own financial outcome. Put your financial requirements above your emotional need to win the approval of professionals and continue working with them, when their most basic function is to serve you. Choose to work with the most qualified and effective financial professional who is willing to take you on as a client. Engage a life coach to establish your Life Goals, Hopes, and Dreams, and a financial professional to align your assets to realize them.

Lastly, congratulations!! Your journey to retirement has not been easy. Whether you have had relatively few or many struggles, or have been less or more "fortunate," you have worked hard and deserve what you have earned. Maximize this capstone of your life, doing what you enjoy most with those you love the most while making it AMAZING, fulfilling your Core Soul Needs — Identity, Life Purpose, Love, and Peace. By Bringing Your Money to Life to live your Life Goals, Hopes and Dreams, you truly are MaxAMAZING Your Retirement. Best wishes!

Endnotes

1   Loving yourself and being loved by yourself are different concepts for a healthy and powerful appreciation of who you are. Loving yourself is actively knowing yourself and what you need for yourself — whether it is to grow in a Facet of Life, modify something about your life, or even give things up that do not fit with who you are Becoming. Being loved by yourself is a passive self-acceptance, recognizing you do not need to stretch into a mold that is not you. It's more than "okay" for you to be your Identity; you need to embrace who you are.

2   At one time, a "financial advisor" was a stringent classification for an individual who was a fee-based planner having a fiduciary obligation. That standard was invalidated as brokerage firms replaced the title of their "brokers" who simply sold investments with the more prestigious title of

"financial advisor." Today, the term "financial advisor" is a generic term that conveys little about the skills or credentialing of the professional or whether the individual has a fiduciary obligation to clients. I prefer the term "Retiree Advisor" for myself because it expresses my approach to advise and coach retirees about their life and money in retirement, and not just offering financial advice disconnected from their Identity and Life Purpose.

3   A "fiduciary" should not be confused with a financial professional who is acting in the best interest of a client but does not meet the regulatory standard of a fiduciary. Fiduciaries place their client's interests above their own and disclose any conflicts of interest. Some fiduciaries also provide fee-based services which not all advisors who act in the best interest of a client are licensed to offer.

Questions for Reflection

- Which of the concept(s) that you have been introduced to through this book have you found to be the most beneficial? The most insightful? The most challenging? The most objectionable? What would you like to spend more time thinking about?

- Have you been spending your life trying to meet the objectives of others and win their approval (or perhaps win your own approval)? Do you feel good about who you are?

- Are the people you are doing life with contributing to both an enjoyable and fulfilling life? With whom might you like to discuss what you read or learned about yourself?

- Are you satisfied with the personal growth you are experiencing? Might it be helpful to consider connecting with a life coach or counselor if you don't have one? If you work with a financial professional, does the planning involve your Identity and Life Purpose and lead to funding and living your Life Goals, Hopes, and Dreams? Considering just the financial aspect of your dealings, are you getting the results you need or might you be guilty of misplaced loyalty and prioritizing the comradery of the relationship over your financial outcomes?

- Have you established your Life Goals, Hopes, and Dreams, and are you living them? If not, what do you need to do to discover who you are and what is most important for you to live in your life?

Glossary

Accomplishments Apex: one of three categories of Life Goals, Hopes, and Dreams that focus on exceptionally meaningful achievements that are closely tied to the Identity/Life Purpose Leg but also build the Love/Peace Leg.

Apex: categories of Fulfillment Life Goals, Hopes, and Dreams that provide enjoyment and fulfillment by meeting Core Soul Needs: Experiences and Relationships, Accomplishments, or Impact.

Apex Legs: a pairing Identity with Life Purpose (Core Souls Needs) and Love with Peace (Core Soul Needs); both pairs are both needed to build Life Goals, Hopes, and Dreams Apexes.

Bad Life Event: an unfortunate life circumstance that has a catastrophic economic impact, either reducing income or increasing expense, threatening the financial stability of survivors.

Becoming: the process of personal growth resulting from building into your Beliefs/Values/Character and Identity Components that you desire to develop into a more important part of your Complete Identity.

Beliefs/Values/Character: what you are confident is true and is important to you, reflected by your moral and ethical views that influence what you prioritize, your preferences, what you are like, and how you do life; it filters everything before you accept it as part of your life.

Bringing Your Money to Life™: a financial planning strategy that and aligns your money with the Financial Destinations that Empower your Life Goals, Hopes, and Dreams.

Capstone: the crowning achievement of your life, where everything you have done has led to who you have become and prepared you to make your retirement both enjoyable and fulfilling, while still leaving you room for additional growth.

Chief Identity Component: your dominant Identity Component or an aspect of your Beliefs/Values/Character that several Identity Components cluster around, that you pursue most often and with the greatest intensity. It tends to be the focus of your thoughts, where you prefer to spend your time and how you meet your emotional needs.

Circumstantial Peace: a feeling that all is well because of the calmness of surrounding life conditions, absent from chaos and strife.

Complete Identity: the "real you" comprised by the totality of your multiple Identity Components, all consistent with your Beliefs/Values/Character.

Core Soul Need: the deepest cries of your heart, which must be met in a meaningful way for you to be fulfilled; consisting of your Identity, Life Purpose, Love, and Peace.

Descriptors: things that say something about you, but you have not internalized and are not part of your Identity.

Disposition Allocation Approach: a financial strategy using instruments acquired for the specific Financial Output they produce for Financial Destinations needed to Empower Life Goals, Hopes, and Dreams.

Empower: when the Financial Destinations of your money fund your Life Goals, Hopes, and Dreams.

Enduring Relationship: a significantly deep emotional connection between individuals sharing common Beliefs/Values/Character, marked by an intentional commitment and concern for each other.

Enjoyment Life Goals, Hopes, and Dreams: a spectacular level of enjoyment you would like to experience that may have been something you have always wanted to do or a fairly recent desire you have set your mind on to live; if structured to meet your Core Soul Needs, it can also be fulfilling.

Expedient Relationship: A link with others providing practical benefits with limited expectations and requirements, that is maintained by automatic points of contact.

Experiences and Relationships Apex: one of three categories of Life Goals, Hopes, and Dreams that focus on enjoying life with those we have meaningful relationships with that is closely tied to the Love/Peace Leg but also build the Identity/Life Purpose Leg.

External Leading: an intuition that you have a "calling" you sense is a plan for your life that you must do.

Facets of Life: a framework consisting of multiple categories for structuring the seemingly unlimited variety of activities you may want to spend your time doing.

Feed: the effect of building an Identity Component through repeated actions of corresponding Facets of Life.

Financial Destinations: how money winds up being used, which can Empower Life Goals, Hopes, and Dreams.

Financial Output: the beneficial results financial instruments are designed to deliver (Income, Growth, Legacy, and Security) that can be Directed Toward Financial Destinations (Spend, Accumulate, Transfer, and Protect).

Fulfillment Life Goals, Hopes, and Dreams: whatever means more to you than anything else that you would really, really enjoy and make your life as fulfilling as it can be by meeting your Core Soul Needs; classified by three Apexes: Experiences and Relationship, Accomplishments, and Impact.

Identity: beliefs and values you developed over time that shaped your character, combined with the Identity Components you internalized.

Identity Components: various aspects of who you are that you express by what you do.

Impact Apex: one of three categories of Life Goals, Hopes, and Dreams that focus on integrating both making a difference in the world, closely tied to the Identity/Life Purpose Leg, and having meaningful relationships, closely tied to the Love/Peace Leg.

Internal Longing: a deep desire that reflects your Identity and triggers your passion for something you want to do in your life.

Investment Allocation Approach: a somewhat indirect and imprecise financial strategy using investments for Growth to Accumulate wealth that will meet all lifetime financial requirements and fund Financial Destinations as needed to Empower Life Goals, Hopes, and Dreams.

Life Goals, Hopes, and Dreams: the pinnacles of your life that are the biggest "WOW" moments, where maximizing your enjoyment can intersect with experiencing amazing fulfillment when meeting your Core Soul Needs.

Life/Money System: an approach to the Realizement stage in life where money is aligned with whatever is most important to you that provides enjoyment and fulfillment to live your Life Goals, Hopes, and Dreams.

Life Purpose: the meaningful connection between your unique Identity and the world around you by what you do that is fulfilling to you and makes a difference for others; "the reason you're on this earth" and how you make the world a better place.

Life Track: personal preparedness to make a smooth transition from being employed to retired, maintaining a meaningful Identity; consisting of Enjoyment and Fulfillment Lanes.

Love: a mutually nurturing relationship between individuals who value and accept one another; they express and receive emotional connectedness that centers on genuine care and affection, characterized by faith, trust, and generosity (as understood by the Greek word "phileo").

Maximizing Enjoyment: doing what you enjoy the most with those you love the most.

Money Track: financial preparation to have sufficient income and assets and perhaps insurance protection to meet your needs throughout retirement.

Peace Partners: individuals you do life with who shower you with emotional wellness by integrating hope with reality and helping you meet our Peace (Core Soul Need).

Peace Stealers: circumstances in life that have the effect of removing a sense of peace and wellbeing.

Pie-Chart Strategy: an Investment Allocation Approach using an asset model for building wealth based on appropriate risk, without considering when to withdraw assets and from which holdings.

Realizement: a perspective for retirement, making it the Capstone stage in your life journey when you have unlimited discretionary time to enjoy life and pursue your Life Goals, Hopes, and Dreams while Becoming who you want; this definition is reserved for the intentional mindset to make this time enjoyable and fulfilling.

Recreation: participating in pleasurable activities because of the enjoyment they bring or the stimulation and refreshment they provide.

Recreationist: an individual who has increased the importance of the Recreation (Facet of Life) in their life from a Descriptor to a prominent Identity Component, if not their Chief Identity.

Retiree: someone who, by choice or not being able to find suitable employment, has permanently left the workforce and is identified as no longer being employed in a career they identified with.

Retirement: the stage in your life when you stop exchanging time for money and have the freedom and flexibility to do whatever you want with your time. Because of the loss of your work identity, you will be creating, establishing, or shifting your identity.

Transcending Peace: an inner sense of wellness experienced regardless of the circumstances, resulting from a trust and confidence in strength greater than circumstances that will provide abeneficial outcome no matter what happens.

Unlimited Discretionary Time: unrestricted, moment-by-moment flexibility to spend your time on non-essential activities, doing what you want, when you want, because of not having responsibilities and requirements; it is not the same as the expanse of time that dwindles with life expectancy.

Disclaimer: The MaxAMAZING™ Your Retirement Life/Money System is a resource for retirees to get the most from their retirement. It recognizes that retirees are highly diverse. Permanently leaving the workforce may be all they have in common. Observations presented are general and do not apply to every retiree. Financial circumstances, interests, concerns, family situations, etc. are unique to each individual. This book is not intended to instruct individuals how they should structure their lives or finances. None of the information presented is intended to serve as financial or legal advice, and this resource should not be construed as a solicitation. Consult properly skilled and licensed counselors and financial professionals regarding your specific situation. Leonard P. ("Len") Hayduchok is a Certified Life Coach and a Certified Financial Planner® practitioner. Len is an investment adviser representative of SGL Financial, LLC, an SEC registered advisory firm. Insurance products and services are offered through individually licensed and appointed agents in appropriate jurisdictions. Leonard Hayduchok NJ License #9243813, Dedicated Financial Services LLC NJ License #1663601, Leonard Hayduchok, DE License # 1331748; Dedicated Financial Services LLC, DE License # 3000323897.

Made in the USA
Middletown, DE
16 May 2023